Suicide

Other Books of Related Interest

Opposing Viewpoints Series

Eating Disorders

Self Mutilation

Violence

Current Controversies Series

Mental Health

Prescription Drugs

Suicide

At Issue Series

Are Americans Overmedicated?

Physician-Assisted Suicide

School Shootings

"Congress shall make no law . . . abridging the freedom of speech, or of the press."

First Amendment to the U.S. Constitution

The basic foundation of our democracy is the First Amendment guarantee of freedom of expression. The Opposing Viewpoints Series is dedicated to the concept of this basic freedom and the idea that it is more important to practice it than to enshrine it.

OPPOSING
VIEWPOINTS®
SERIES

Suicide

Jacqueline Langwith, Book Editor

GREENHAVEN PRESS
A part of Gale, Cengage Learning

GALE
CENGAGE Learning™

Detroit • New York • San Francisco • New Haven, Conn • Waterville, Maine • London

GALE
CENGAGE Learning·

Christine Nasso, *Publisher*
Elizabeth Des Chenes, *Managing Editor*

© 2008 Greenhaven Press, a part of Gale, Cengage Learning.

Gale and Greenhaven Press are registered trademarks used herein under license.

For more information, contact:
Greenhaven Press
27500 Drake Rd.
Farmington Hills, MI 48331-3535
Or you can visit our Internet site at gale.cengage.com

Articles in Greenhaven Press anthologies are often edited for length to meet page requirements. In addition, original titles of these works are changed to clearly present the main thesis and to explicitly indicate the author's opinion. Every effort is made to ensure that Greenhaven Press accurately reflects the original intent of the authors. Every effort has been made to trace the owners of copyrighted material.

Cover photograph reproduced by permission of Ellicott Davies/Stone/Getty Images.

LIBRARY OF CONGRESS CATALOGING-IN-PUBLICATION DATA

Suicide / Jacqueline Langwith, book editor.
    p. cm. -- (Opposing viewpoints)
    Includes bibliographical references and index.
    ISBN 978-0-7377-4012-7 (hardcover)
    ISBN 978-0-7377-4013-4 (pbk.)
    1. Suicide. 2. Suicide--Prevention. 3. Assisted suicide. I. Langwith, Jacqueline.
    HV6545.S8182 2008
    362.28--dc22

                          2008001007

Printed in the United States of America
2 3 4 5 6 7 12 11 10 09 08

Contents

Chapter 3: How Can Suicide Be Prevented?

Why Consider
Opposing Viewpoints?

> *"The only way in which a human being can make some approach to knowing the whole of a subject is by hearing what can be said about it by persons of every variety of opinion and studying all modes in which it can be looked at by every character of mind. No wise man ever acquired his wisdom in any mode but this."*
>
> John Stuart Mill

In our media-intensive culture it is not difficult to find differing opinions. Thousands of newspapers and magazines and dozens of radio and television talk shows resound with differing points of view. The difficulty lies in deciding which opinion to agree with and which "experts" seem the most credible. The more inundated we become with differing opinions and claims, the more essential it is to hone critical reading and thinking skills to evaluate these ideas. Opposing Viewpoints books address this problem directly by presenting stimulating debates that can be used to enhance and teach these skills. The varied opinions contained in each book examine many different aspects of a single issue. While examining these conveniently edited opposing views, readers can develop critical thinking skills such as the ability to compare and contrast authors' credibility, facts, argumentation styles, use of persuasive techniques, and other stylistic tools. In short, the Opposing Viewpoints Series is an ideal way to attain the higher-level thinking and reading skills so essential in a culture of diverse and contradictory opinions.

In addition to providing a tool for critical thinking, Opposing Viewpoints books challenge readers to question their own strongly held opinions and assumptions. Most people form their opinions on the basis of upbringing, peer pressure, and personal, cultural, or professional bias. By reading carefully balanced opposing views, readers must directly confront new ideas as well as the opinions of those with whom they disagree. This is not to simplistically argue that everyone who reads opposing views will—or should—change his or her opinion. Instead, the series enhances readers' understanding of their own views by encouraging confrontation with opposing ideas. Careful examination of others' views can lead to the readers' understanding of the logical inconsistencies in their own opinions, perspective on why they hold an opinion, and the consideration of the possibility that their opinion requires further evaluation.

Evaluating Other Opinions

To ensure that this type of examination occurs, Opposing Viewpoints books present all types of opinions. Prominent spokespeople on different sides of each issue as well as well-known professionals from many disciplines challenge the reader. An additional goal of the series is to provide a forum for other, less known, or even unpopular viewpoints. The opinion of an ordinary person who has had to make the decision to cut off life support from a terminally ill relative, for example, may be just as valuable and provide just as much insight as a medical ethicist's professional opinion. The editors have two additional purposes in including these less known views. One, the editors encourage readers to respect others' opinions—even when not enhanced by professional credibility. It is only by reading or listening to and objectively evaluating others' ideas that one can determine whether they are worthy of consideration. Two, the inclusion of such viewpoints encourages the important critical thinking skill of objectively evaluating an author's credentials and bias. This evaluation will illuminate an author's reasons for taking a particular stance on an issue and will aid in readers' evaluation of the author's ideas.

It is our hope that these books will give readers a deeper understanding of the issues debated and an appreciation of the complexity of even seemingly simple issues when good and honest people disagree. This awareness is particularly important in a democratic society such as ours in which people enter into public debate to determine the common good. Those with whom one disagrees should not be regarded as enemies but rather as people whose views deserve careful examination and may shed light on one's own.

Thomas Jefferson once said that "difference of opinion leads to inquiry, and inquiry to truth." Jefferson, a broadly educated man, argued that "if a nation expects to be ignorant and free ... it expects what never was and never will be." As individuals and as a nation, it is imperative that we consider the opinions of others and examine them with skill and discernment. The Opposing Viewpoints Series is intended to help readers achieve this goal.

David L. Bender and Bruno Leone,
Founders

Introduction

> "... During the first couple of months after my sister's suicide, we talked about her incessantly. We reminisced about how she acted and looked. We had an insatiable desire to reconstruct the weeks before she died. We recounted the last conversations, moods, phone calls, photographs and meals, hoping that somehow our memories would explain the answer to why she'd killed herself. That question still gnawed at our guts, creating a big, black, empty hole...."
>
> —Debbie,
> Suicide Survivor, American Foundation
> for Suicide Prevention

Why do people kill themselves? This difficult question plagues the loved ones who suicide victims leave behind. Very often they feel guilt or shame: Why didn't they recognize the signs? How could they not have known the despair their loved one felt? Unfortunately, for the loved ones of suicide victims, there is no easy answer to the question of why someone kills himself or herself.

Science also has attempted to understand the motives behind suicide. For many years, the decision of ending one's own life has intrigued scientists. Several theories have been put forth. In the late 19th century, a theory of suicide was offered by one of the founding fathers of sociology. Later, a theory was formulated by a preeminent psychologist. More recently, biological theories have been put forth that try to link suicide to particular genes or neurotransmitter levels in the brain.

In the late 19th century, a French scientist named Emile Durkheim performed a revolutionary study. Durkheim studied the suicide rates of people based on their marital status, whether or not they had children, and on their religion. He found that suicide rates were higher for unmarried people, those without children, and for Protestants. Based on these findings, he devised a sociological theory to explain why people committed suicide. Durkheim's theory was contained in a classic book entitled *Suicide* that was published in 1897. The book was groundbreaking for several reasons. It represented the first published work in the just-emerging field of sociology. By showing how the individual act of suicide could be influenced by society, Durkheim proved the usefulness of sociology. Additionally, his method of collecting data about a small group of people, i.e. those who had committed suicide, and then looking at what the data told him, represents the first use of the "case study" method of sociological research. Emile Durkheim is one of the founding fathers of the field of sociology, and his book *Suicide* is a classic work that is still read by sociologists today.

In *Suicide*, Durkheim asserted that suicide is a consequence of social factors. According to Durkheim, people have a certain level of attachment to their social groups, which he called social integration. Abnormally low or high levels of social integration may result in increased suicide rates. People who feel isolated or alienated from society have high levels of suicide, as do people who have extremely intense social connections. The former group turns to suicide as a last resort, while the latter group kills themselves to avoid being a burden on society. Durkheim found that Catholics had lower suicide rates than Protestants because Catholics tended to have stronger social networks. Married persons and people with children also had lower rates of suicide. Durkheim found that healthy social relationships provided in marriage and parenthood had a protective effect on suicide. Durkheim's sociological theory of suicide is still taught in sociology courses.

Clinical psychologist Edwin Shneidman's interest in suicide began about fifty years after Durkheim published *Suicide*. In 1949, Shneidman visited a Los Angeles coroner's office while investigating the suicides of two men. The suicide note left behind by one of the men gave Shneidman the idea that by analyzing the notes of other suicide victims, he might be able to find common clues as to why they had decided to end their lives. So, Shneidman and his colleague collected and analyzed hundreds of suicide notes. He concluded that suicide results from "psychache," a word he coined to describe the unbearable psychological pain arising from unmet psychological needs. "There is no suicide without a great deal of psychological pain," said Shneidman. Based on his analysis, Shneidman developed a list of characteristics that are commonly associated with completed suicides. He found that the common purpose of suicide is to seek a solution, and the common goal of suicide is to end consciousness and thereby put an end to feelings of shame, guilt, anger, fear, and sadness. The common emotions of suicide are hopelessness and helplessness. Suicidal people have an overwhelming feeling of hopelessness and are sure that nothing can be done to improve their lives, hence suicide is the only option. According to Shneidman, while there is a sincere wish to end their pain, there is also a longing for an alternative to suicide. However, the person is unable to see the alternatives. Schneidman's list of characteristics of suicidal people is still used by psychiatrists today.

Some fifty years after Shneidman developed his theory of suicide and nearly a hundred years after Durkheim's book *Suicide* was published, researchers are trying to discern the biological basis of suicide. Since 2002, scientist John Mann from Columbia University has contributed a significant amount of information about the connection between brain chemistry and suicide. Much like Durkheim's case study and

Shneidman's suicide notes, Mann assembled a collection of data and then looked at what the data was telling him about suicide. Mann's data however, is much different than either Durkheim's or Shneidman's, as it comes in the form of brain specimens. Stored in several deep freezers in Mann's laboratory are two hundred gelatinous brain specimens from people who have committed suicide. Along with each brain is a set of case notes, including interviews with family members, to show the victim's state of mind and behavior before they took their lives.

What Mann and his colleagues have found so far is that suicide is associated with low serotonin levels in a certain part of the brain. Serotonin is a neurotransmitter that plays a part in virtually every thought and feeling we have. According to Mann, "feeling suicidal is just a very sad and terrible feeling." Mann and his colleagues found that suicidal behavior involves low serotonin levels in a very small part of the brain in the prefrontal cortex. This is the decision-making part of the brain. "The story with suicidal behavior is that, in a particular area of the brain, this decision making area of the brain, they've got low serotonin function. So that if they get depressed and they feel suicidal, or if they get angry and they want to hit somebody, they are more likely to do it," says Mann. Mann and other researchers also have found that there may be a gene that predisposes people to suicide. The children of suicide attempters are six times more likely to attempt suicide than the children of nonsuicide attempters. Researchers have not yet been able to identify a suicide-causing gene, however.

As Durkheim, Shneidman, and Mann have found, suicide is a complex human behavior that no single theory can explain. However, there is hope that someday scientists can better understand the basis for suicide. If they can, the suicides of many people may be prevented, and the grief of their loved ones can be spared. In *Opposing Viewpoints: Suicide*, the contributors explore the issues of suicide in the following chapters: Who Is Most At Risk for Suicide? What Are Some of the Causes of Suicide? How Can Suicide Be Prevented? And, Should Doctor-Assisted Suicide Be Allowed?

OPPOSING
VIEWPOINTS®
SERIES

CHAPTER 1

Who Is Most at Risk for Suicide?

Chapter Preface

Cindy lives in Los Angeles and is sixteen. Her short, spiky hair is dyed jet black. Her nose, lips, and ears are pierced, and she wears a chain around her neck. She dresses in black clothes every day and wears black lipstick and dark eyeliner. She is sensitive, moody, artistic, introspective, and tolerant of others. She is drawn to dark music and literature. Her clothing and appearance say "look at me," but she is not comfortable in public. Cindy is a part of the Goth subculture, an often-troubled teen social group. Kids like Cindy live in small towns and big cities across the United States.

There is some indication that the Goth subculture may exert a negative influence on teens like Cindy that increases their risk of suicide. However, it is also possible that troubled teens are drawn to the Goth subculture, and the group actually provides social connections that decrease their suicide risk.

It is not easy to define the Goth subculture. Goth emerged from the defiant punk music scene in the United Kingdom during the late 1970s and early 1980s. A 2006 article in the *London Sunday Times* discussing Goth bands the Horrors and Betty Curse says "anti-conformism is the thread that runs through Goth's various strands. Goth is anti-straight, anti-religious, and anti-corporate." According to the Web site, www.goth.net, the question: "What is Goth?" is probably the hardest question any Goth could try and answer. "One may as well ask 'what is society?' as it has so many facets it defies any definitive explanation." The Web site goes on to say that, "Goth is a group of people who feel comfortable within each other's company," and except for the wearing of black, "there is no specific thing that defines what you need to do or be to fit into the Goth scene." Lisa and Andrew from http://anon.razor wire.com say, "a Goth is somebody who listens to Gothic music and looks Gothic."

Goths tend to be associated with sadness and depression. Psychologists who council adolescents say they treat a disproportionately large number of Goth teens for depression and self-harming behaviors. Clinical psychologist Wendy Lader of the organization S.A.F.E. (Self Abuse Finally Ends) Alternatives believes that self-harming behaviors are an accepted part of the "Goth" subculture. Says Lader, "I think kids in the Goth movement are looking for something, some acceptance in an alternative culture. And self-injury is definitely a coping strategy for unhappy kids." The Web site www.gothicrevue.com says that depression seems to be a feeling that Goth personifies. "Subcultures take an idea and exaggerate it to the point where they typify it. This exaggeration of the beauty of sadness in Gothic culture leads people to think that Goths are more depressed than other groups." The Web site goes on to say, "it is possible that Goths are more depressed than other people. It is also possible that this is just the impression people get about Gothic because it is an exaggerated personification."

A research study seems to back up the notion that Goths are depressed and at risk for suicide. In 2006, researchers in Scotland reported a link between Goth subculture and suicide. The researchers surveyed a group of more than twelve-thousand kids at age eleven, and then again at thirteen, fifteen, and nineteen years old. The kids were asked whether they belonged to any social group and whether they had ever attempted to harm themselves, including by cutting and by attempting suicide. According to the researchers, about half of the nineteen-year-olds who identified themselves as being Goth had attempted suicide or had an incident of self-harm in their lives. The researchers said that Goth teens were fourteen times more likely to harm themselves and sixteen times more likely to attempt suicide than kids in the general population. Being Goth was a stronger predictor for suicide than being depressed, using drugs, or having divorced parents.

The study was picked up by the media and widely reported. "Goth Teens More Likely to Kill Selves," or "Half of Young Goths Have Tried Suicide," read the headlines. However, many people, including the lead researcher of the study, cautioned against drawing too broad a conclusion from the results. Robert Young from the University of Glasgow, who led the research study, said that the study does not make clear whether Goth culture leads to self-destructive behavior or whether teens with those tendencies gravitate to Goth. Most of the teens that attempted suicide or harmed themselves did so *before* joining the Goth subculture. "Rather than posing a risk, it's also possible that by belonging to this subculture young people are gaining valuable social and emotional support from their peers," said Young. Gregory Fritz, a professor of psychiatry at Brown University agrees. He says, "the Goth subculture may be an important, accepting social support for an otherwise isolated group of teenagers."

Both professors favor more research. According to Young, "before any conclusions can be reached about Goth teens and suicide, more studies are needed." Fritz urges mental health professionals not to jump to any conclusions, but to be aware that Goths may have an increased suicide risk. Says Fritz, "until the definitive study becomes available, mental health professionals do well to approach the teenage Goth with concern but evaluate each on an individual basis."

Whether being Goth leads to depression and suicide, or whether Goth membership provides protection against suicide, is an important topic of debate. Knowing the underlying suicide risk of vulnerable groups of people can be the beginning of getting them the help they need. In the following chapter, the contributors discuss the suicide risk of other groups of people in the United States.

> *"The adolescent may feel they have no choice but to end their intense internal suffering or to solve a hopeless dilemma by ending it all."*

Teens Are Particularly at Risk for Suicide

Michael S. Jellinek

In the following viewpoint, Michael Jellinek asserts that adolescents are particularly vulnerable to suicide. Adolescence is a time of great change and a sense of loss, says Jellinek. Incidents such as the break-up of a relationship or receiving a college rejection letter, combined with depression, and increasing alcohol consumption cause many teens to attempt suicide or engage in risky life-threatening behavior. Sadly, says Jellinek, there isn't always a way to prevent teen suicide. However, he offers several suggestions that may help, such as talking to teens and helping them cope with difficult situations. Michael Jellinek is a child psychiatrist and a professor of psychiatry and pediatrics at Harvard Medical School.

As you read, consider the following questions:

1. According to Jellinek, what is the leading cause of adolescent death?

2. What percentage of high school students had seriously considered attempting suicide, according to statistics from a 2001 Centers for Disease Control and Prevention survey?

3. According to Jellinek, in what percentage of suicide cases do adolescents not display obvious outward signs of anguish?

Adolescent suicide is a matter of deep concern for anyone who cares about children: their families, their teachers and counselors, their friends.

As pediatricians, the thought of one of our patients taking their own life by overt suicide or an "accident" resulting from foolish, high-risk behavior causes us deep-felt anxiety. It seems, on the surface, to be so preventable. However, the sad truth is that knowing which teenager is truly suicidal or about to take a terrible risk, controlling that behavior—even for a few days—and preventing the tragic loss of a young life are all very difficult, and sometimes impossible, judgments and tasks.

We get anxious whenever we are expected, or expect ourselves, to do the impossible.

High-Risk Behavior

Suicide constitutes the third leading cause of death in 10- to 19-year-olds, accounting for 1,921 deaths in 2002, the latest year for which figures are available. Suicide is less common in children ages 10–14, with 300 children in this age group taking their own lives in 2002. Still, it is a sobering thought that the suicide rate among younger children has risen 70% since 1981.

The leading cause of adolescent death, of course, is accidents: motor vehicle accidents, firearms accidents, dives, falls, and the like, many spurred on by alcohol, drugs, and excessive speed.

Clearly, a lot of risk-taking behavior drives these statistics, and I would like to ask you to consider whether a certain amount of overlap may exist between suicides and accidents fueled by high-risk life-threatening behavior.

The Centers for Disease Control and Prevention's Youth Risk Behavior Surveillance survey in 2001 found that 19% of high school students had seriously considered attempting suicide; 15% had made plans, and 9% attempted suicide. How many of these same teenagers died in "accidents" in ensuing years when their cars slammed into trees at high speed, or they dove into a quarry at night after drinking 10 beers?

Adolescence Brings Change and Sense of Loss

Adolescence is a time of major change in the life of an individual, a time of developing identity and autonomy, discovering one's skills and limitations, engaging in intense peer relationships, and shifting one's focus away from parents and family to the future: leaving home and entering the adult world.

While adolescence is exciting, there is inherently a sense of loss entwined in adolescence. Physically and cognitively, privacy becomes increasingly relevant.

But congratulatory rituals, such as high school graduation and "prom night," accentuate very publicly the approaching loss of a familiar community, school, and friends, even as they reflect great accomplishment and adventure.

At the same time, adolescents overestimate their abilities. If they did not, would they be eager to apply to college, enter the military, or apply for a job? They have great confidence in their driving skills, for example, and they often set unrealistic expectations for themselves, such as playing professional sports while they sit on the bench of their high school varsity team, or making it to the big screen as an actor after being a cast member in the school play.

If you combine a sense of loss with the notion that you can pull off more than you really can, suddenly you find yourself in the song lyrics of the movie "Fame": "I'm going to live forever. I'm going to learn how to fly."

What may bring them thudding back to Earth may be something that seems to us not such a big deal—a "D" on an important exam, not making a team, the breakup of a high school relationship, rejection of a college application—or it may be more substantial: their parents divorce or the loss of a close friend. These real losses may be complicated by a biological vulnerability to depression, and the losses may come at a time when the adolescent's experiments with drugs or weekend drinking is moving from occasional to a pattern or habit.

Sudden and Overwhelming Despair

Many adolescents lack a realistic sense of the longer term, the idea that tomorrow is another day, that they have the power to recover.

Their despair may be sudden and overwhelming, even when they have not previously shown signs of depression or difficulties in managing their schoolwork, friendships, and family life, or may compound a tendency toward . . . depression. Having "failed," with no discernible way to save face or grasp a second chance, the adolescent may feel they have no choice but to end their intense internal suffering or to solve a hopeless dilemma by ending it all.

Being depressed, sustaining a series of blows, and being under the influence of alcohol multiply the sense of being trapped, hopeless, and helpless. At these moments, the adolescent's intellectual understanding of death as permanent may regress as they find emotional comfort in fantasizing the

Youth Suicide Facts

- Each year, there are approximately 10 youth suicides for every 100,000 youth.

- Each day, there are approximately 12 youth suicides.

- Every 2 hours and 11 minutes, a person under the age of 25 completes suicide.

- In 2004, 32,439 people completed suicide. Of these, 4,316 were completed by people between the ages of 15 and 24. . . .

- Research has shown that most adolescent suicides occur after school hours and in the teen's home.

- Although rates vary somewhat by geographic location, within a typical high school classroom, it is likely that three students (one boy and two girls) have made a suicide attempt in the past year.

- The typical profile of an adolescent nonfatal suicide attempter is a female who ingests pills, while the profile of the typical suicide completer is a male who dies from a gunshot wound.

- Not all adolescent attempters may admit their intent. Therefore, any deliberate self-harming behaviors should be considered serious and in need of further evaluation.

American Association of Suicidology,
"Youth Suicide Fact Sheet," December 28, 2006. Available at:
www.suicidology.org/associations/1045/files/Youth2004.pdf

scene after they're dead: the boyfriend or girlfriend finally realizing how much they loved them or the rejecting parent now feeling terrible guilt.

This complex developmental vulnerability explains why so often adolescent suicide takes us all so horribly by surprise. In 10%–30% of cases of suicide, and probably a much higher percentage of serious "accidents," adolescents do not display obvious outward signs of anguish. Everybody's blind-sided. They wonder, how could we have not seen that this person was so miserable, so vulnerable, that he or she could take such a drastic step, or make a fatal misjudgment?

Limitations to Prevention

It is hard to accept our limitations as pediatricians, grieving parents, or distraught school counselors. In these circumstances, there probably wasn't much to see that distinguished this teenager's suffering and dilemmas from any others—and there was little if anything that could have been done.

Recognizing our limitations should not make us feel "hopeless and helpless." We must all be on the lookout for signs of major depression in a teen with a personal or family history of depression, and/or substance abuse. We need to be aware of risk-taking behavior, of the teen who has too many eggs in one basket and is at risk for a crushing disappointment, or a teen who seems too isolated.

Always speak to adolescents privately when they come to your office. Try to gain a sense of whether they feel connected to something: a team, their school, and family. Do they have somewhat reasonable hopes and dreams? A person who they trust and who they see as tolerant?

Even when outward signs of despair are not present, remember that anxiety may be most pronounced at vulnerable times during adolescence: early puberty and times of emerging sexual identity; the period during junior and senior years when students apply to college; prom; graduation.

In any patient who you feel may be unusually vulnerable to suicide or high-risk, suicidal behavior, be very concerned. Try to assess whether he or she has considered suicide, whether plans have been made, and whether the adolescent has ready access to the means of suicide. By all means, enlist help from mental health professionals if necessary.

How to Help

How does one prevent suicide in a teenager who displays no signs of depression or difficulty coping with life's troubles? Quite humbly, beyond minimizing access to firearms and drugs with lethal potential, I do not know.

As a child psychiatrist and a father, I do think it is important to talk through tough problems with an adolescent, using scenarios from real life, the movies, or TV. I'll say, "What do you think that kid should have done?" "What options did she have?" And of course I try to maintain a deep feeling of connection, without excessive control.

Learning to deal with life's rough turns takes practice.

Help them learn how to consider possible solutions to thorny dilemmas, how to access help, and how to see beyond the angst of the moment.

I can't prove this is an effective strategy in helping to avert suicides and serious accidents among teens: certainly there's little evidence-based medicine to guide us here. But it is the best I have to offer.

"Teen suicide, a tragedy in any single instance, is magnified many times over in the Native American community."

Native American Teens Are Most at Risk for Suicide

Native American Report

In the following viewpoint, the journal Native American Report *explores the 2005 hearing on Native American teen suicide held by the U.S. Senate Indian Affairs Committee. The article contends that there is a teen suicide epidemic in Native American tribal communities. A big part of the problem, according to the article, is that most tribal communities lack mental health resources and constructive activities for youths. Federal funding for reservation-based mental health services, recreation programs, teen centers, and prevention programs is needed to reduce the alarming teen suicide rate in Native American communities.* Native American Report *is a monthly publication providing information about federal activities that affect Native American tribal communities.*

As you read, consider the following questions:

1. According to *Native American Report*, Native American children under the age of fifteen are how many times more likely than other children to take their own life?

2. According to *Native American Report*, how far do teens of the Standing Rock Sioux Tribe in North and South Dakota have to drive in order to talk to a counselor?

3. According to *Native American Report*, what percentage of the Native population nationwide lives in poverty?

Teen suicide, a tragedy in any single instance, is magnified many times over in the Native American community, where poverty, alcohol abuse and other social ills push a disproportionately high number of teens over the brink.

Training a spotlight on the issue, the U.S. Congress Senate Indian Affairs Committee last month [June 2005] held the first Capitol Hill hearing on the subject, following a field hearing in North Dakota the month before.

Native Americans in general have the highest suicide rate of any ethnic group in the U.S., and Native children under age 15 are five times more likely to take their own life than are other children that age, according to Sen. Byron Dorgan, the ranking Democrat on the Indian Affairs Committee.

"This epidemic is not limited to one tribe or one reservation. It is happening in tribal communities across the nation," said Dorgan.

Suicide ranks second in cause of death for American Indians and Alaska Natives ages 15 to 24, according to statistics cited at the hearings.

Youths ages 15 to 24 make up 40 percent of all suicides in Indian Country, according to Surgeon General Richard Carmona. And, he said, those numbers are just the tip of the iceberg: for each fatality, some 13 nonfatal events occur.

Growing Problem

Unfortunately, the trend is worsening, Carmona said, with suicide and suicidal behavior becoming more prevalent in many smaller tribal communities. This is occurring at a time when the nation's overall suicide rate is declining, he noted.

Carmona said more research and intervention are needed to understand the problem and develop solutions. The administration's fiscal year 2006 budget request includes a $4.3 million, or 8 percent, increase to $59 million for mental health programs of the Indian Health Service, he said.

"As sensitive as the topic is, we can't put off dealing with the issue of suicide, particularly among teenagers, on our reservations," said Dorgan. "We need to address the root causes, the assistance that's available to troubled teens, and the funding and human resources that are needed to reverse this devastating trend."

Reservations Lack Mental Health Professionals

One of the biggest problems, cited both by Dorgan and witnesses testifying at the hearings, is the lack of available mental health professionals on reservations—and the distances that residents have to travel to see those that are available.

For example, it is a 40- to 75-mile trip to get to the nearest counseling for members of the Standing Rock Sioux Tribe in North and South Dakota, according to Twila Rough Surface, who testified before the committee about the devastating effects of teen suicide.

Last winter, Rough Surface lost a niece to suicide, in a tragedy that led her sister to attempt suicide. This all followed the loss of her nephew in a car accident, an event that led the boy's best friend to commit suicide.

"At no point did any mental health professional contact our family," said Rough Surface. "I feel if there had been intervention with grief counseling and support for my sister and her children, my niece may have had a chance to grow to be an elder of the community."

But with high poverty rates, lack of suicide prevention programs and limited access to counseling, few tribe members can get the help they need, she said.

Some New Projects Filling the Gap

While still limited in number, suicide prevention and mental health programs are stepping into the breach on several reservations.

The Cheyenne River Youth Project in Eagle Butte, S.D., grew out of tragedy: 17 youths have been lost to suicide in recent years. The project is located in the Northern Plains, where Native youth are often five to seven times more likely to commit suicide, according to Julie Garreau, executive director of the project. Nationwide, Native youth are two to three times more likely to take their own lives than are other youths, she said.

"Cheyenne River has seen a heart-wrenching spate of suicides," she said. And it is not just the suicide clusters that people know about; it is also the three to seven suicide attempts every week on the reservation, she said.

Trying to track the causes, her project surveyed youths, adults and service providers about mental health problems and found these issues at the top: substance abuse, gang activity and violence, lack of youth activities, and negative youth behavior.

All spoke of a need for funding for mental health services, recreational and job opportunities, programs that put adults in contact with youths and prevention programs, Garreau said.

"If we can create a positive outlook for our youth, and programs that have daily contact with our young people, we will be much better prepared to stop this cycle of loss," she said.

In Cheyenne River, one answer is a new teen center, which is expected to open next spring. "With no mall, no movie theater, no bowling alley, few jobs and very long winters, there are very few healthy outlets for our teens," she said. The new teen center will include a library, Internet cafe, basketball courts and Lakota language and arts classes—as well as counseling offices.

Farther to the West is another project aimed at stemming the tide of suicide among Natives: the One Sky Center at Oregon Health & Science University. Run by R. Dale Walker, a Cherokee psychiatrist, One Sky is considered the first national resource center for prevention and treatment of substance abuse and mental health among Native Americans.

Begun in 2003, the center is now in its final year of a grant from the Substance Abuse and Mental Health Services Administration.

Another model, cited by the surgeon general, is the Phoenix Indian Medical Center, which has begun an "Open Access Model of Care," where patients can walk into the behavioral health department without an appointment and see a licensed clinician the same day. That center, Carmona said, sees more than 18,000 patients a year.

In Alaska, a brand new Behavioral Health Aid program trains community members as paraprofessionals to conduct culturally sensitive screening and intervention in small villages, according to Carmona. Able to serve the most isolated and remote populations, "this program is in its infancy but shows substantial promise for long-term success and the possibility of replication across Indian Country," said Carmona.

Reservations Need Federal Services

Walker, as did other witnesses, recommended enhancing mental health services for Native communities, particularly through the pending reauthorization of the Indian Health Care Improvement Act.

No One to Talk to

Michelle Fasthorse is a senior at Standing Rock [Reservation]. She says many teens simply feel like they have no one to talk to. . . .

"I think because we teens are very confused about life and have a lot of stress and pressure on us, we become depressed," said Fasthorse. "Some teens have absolutely no trust in anyone, due to the fact that no one is there for them to talk to. That's probably why they don't talk to counselors and try to get help.". . .

And it's not just teenagers expressing frustration. Dr. Doug McDonald is director of the Indians into Psychology program at the University of North Dakota. He has two decades of experience working on Indian reservations. McDonald says there's a frightening lack of data about American Indian psychosocial behavior.

McDonald says tribes often close their doors to researchers because they've been exploited in the past. He urged tribal leaders to participate in research and treatment based on Indian values.

"Reopening those doors will not be easy. Yet it may become necessary in order to gain a greater understanding of this monstrous problem that is causing our children to believe that a gun or a handful of pills is a more worthwhile option than asking someone to talk," said McDonald. McDonald says he fears a "rising tsunami" of teen suicides on reservations.

Dan Gunderson, "Indian Teen Suicide: A Tragedy of Enormous Proportions," Minnesota Public Radio, May 3, 2005.

"The alarming health disparities, domestic violence, suicide and major crimes committed on Indian reservations are escalating, and show no signs of relenting unless crucial federal programs are fully funded," Walker said.

Walker lauded use of culturally relevant, community-specific approaches for mental health issues, specifically the Community Suicide Prevention Assessment Tool used at One Sky. He also recommended that a long-term intervention program be established for communities that undergo crisis or emergencies.

"The issue of suicide in Indian Country will take years, not months, to address, and just as suicide among American Indian/Alaska Native populations is a multifactorial phenomena, the response must also be multifaceted," said Carmona.

Witness after witness pointed to the desperate economic conditions in Indian Country that lead both youth and adults to despair.

"Tribal families live in a crucible of economic oppression and lack of opportunity," with 26 percent of the Native population nationwide—including 38 percent children—living in poverty, according to Joseph Stone, program manager and clinical supervisor of the Confederated Tribes of the Grande Ronde Behavioral Health Program in Grande Ronde, Ore.

Stone, a licensed psychologist who testified on behalf of the American Psychological Association, said he was exposed "early and frequently" to violent death and suicide as a child raised on a reservation. His brother committed suicide at age 18, as did a close family friend at age 19 and a cousin at age 20, he told the committee.

He pointed to a lack of qualified Native professionals to help and cost issues that prohibit Natives from getting needed help.

> "The preponderance of attention has been given to suicide among men, with relative silence about its impact on women."

Women Are Particularly at Risk for Suicide

Linda H. Chaudron and Eric D. Caine

In the following viewpoint, Linda Chaudron and Eric Caine contend that there is a lack of research into the causes of female suicide. Most research data about suicide risks tend to focus on men since men complete more suicides than women. But say Chaudron and Caine, women are more likely than men to attempt suicide. They review what is known about the risk factors of suicide for women in comparison to men. Linda Chaudron is an assistant professor and Eric Caine is co-director of the Center for the Study and Prevention of Suicide at the University of Rochester School of Medicine.

As you read, consider the following questions:

1. According to the authors, how does Patrick O'Carroll define suicide? How does he define suicide ideation?

Linda H. Chaudron, Eric D. Caine, "Suicide Among Women: A Critical Review," *Journal of the American Medical Women's Association*, vol. 59, Spring, 2004, pp. 125–132. Reproduced by permission. Available at http://www.amwa-doc.org/index.cfm?objectid= 1297D910-D567-0B25-5F32C34C7DDF396C.

2. According to the authors, what is the most robust and compelling finding for men and women who commit suicide?

3. According to the authors, in 2000 what was the most common method of suicide among women?

Suicidology has progressed during the past 2 decades, with the development of psychological autopsies, large national databases, and a national imperative to understand and prevent suicide. Despite its growth, current research contributes little to a comprehensive understanding of the factors that influence suicidal behaviors in women. Before considering the complexities of suicide among women, we must establish *why* it is imperative that researchers, public health advocates, policy makers, and clinicians address this critical issue at both population and individual levels.

Why Study Suicide in Women?

Mortality is measured as the "worst" outcome of disease. Hence, medical research often aims at identifying and combating risk factors for fatal outcomes. Studies that exclude associated morbidity [the rate of incidence on number of attempts, both fatal and non-fatal] fail to capture important sources of disease burden. For example, suicide is the greatest cause of death among psychiatric patients, but it is only the "tip of the iceberg." At its base lies an array of psychiatric and social pathologies that contribute to a range of suicidal behaviors and outcomes.

As the urgency to combat suicide and its antecedent conditions has grown, the preponderance of attention has been given to suicide among men, with relative silence about its impact on women. Suicides among men in the United States outnumber those among women fourfold. When morbidity and mortality are considered together, however, the weight of disease burden shifts heavily toward women. At a minimum, suicide attempts occur 10 times as often as suicide, and women account for the majority of reported attempts. Depression, which is highly prevalent among men and women who commit suicide, disproportionately affects women. It is with this broader perspective that the need to critically study suicide among women becomes clear.

No one understands what factors put some women at greater risk of suicide. What are the similarities or differences between women who kill themselves and those who attempt suicide but do not die? How do these relate to an even broader group who engage in self-injurious behaviors? This paper does not answer these questions but lays the groundwork for future exploration by focusing on data surrounding suicide deaths among women.

In this paper, we briefly review what is known, what is missing, and the practical aspects of assessing women in clinical settings. We focus on suicide in adult women, but draw on available literature about serious attempts. We present studies conducted primarily in the United States, but data from international samples also are considered when relevant. The objectives are to: 1) review current data on rates and risk factors for female suicides gleaned from studies that present sex-specific findings, 2) describe theories for differences between men and women with regard to suicide, 3) discuss the implications for clinical practice, and 4) consider avenues for future research.

Difficulties of Suicide Research

There are many challenges to conducting suicide research, including defining the broad range of suicidal behaviors, overcoming inconsistencies and misclassifications of death certificates and records, and addressing the lack of prospective epidemiological studies among large representative population samples in the United States. Because the rates are relatively low in women compared with men, the hurdles are even higher when conducting research to understand the risk and protective factors for suicide among women.

The inconsistent use of terminology is one problem that must be understood when interpreting the literature. Terms such as suicidal ideation, suicide attempt, and parasuicidal behavior are often misused or combined under the heading "suicidal behaviors." To improve clarity, [Patrick W.] O'Carroll and associates proposed the following commonly used classifications. *Suicide* is "a death from injury, poisoning, or suffocation where there is evidence (either explicit or implicit) that the injury was self-inflicted *and* that the decedent intended to kill himself/herself." *Suicide attempt* is "a potentially self-injurious behavior with a nonfatal outcome, for which there is evidence (either explicit or implicit), that the individual intended at some (nonzero) level to kill himself/herself." *Suicidal ideation* is "any self-reported thoughts of engaging in suicide-related behavior." This paper focuses on suicide as defined above.

Who Are the Women Who Die by Suicide?

The demographic factors most often cited when considering suicide risk are gender, age, race, and marital status. Many clinicians are aware that the demographic factors associated with the highest rates of suicide are being male, white, elderly, and single (divorced/widowed). Although critical, this information has limited applicability to women. Who are the women who die by suicide, and how can we identify those at risk?

According to the Centers for Disease Control and Prevention, the rate of suicide among women in the United States was 4.0 per 100,000 in 2000, which meant that 5732 women died from suicide. This is one-quarter the rate among men (17.1 deaths/100,000 or 23,618 men). This 4:1 ratio has remained constant since 1989 and is consistent with international patterns, with the exception of rural China. A multitude of factors likely contributes to the sex differences in suicide rates. . . .

Suicide rates differ among women by age. The rate of suicide among women ages 20 to 64 declined 16% between 1980 and 1994. Despite the decline, the greatest burden for suicide deaths and the highest rates of suicide are among women between the ages of 35 and 64. This pattern differs from that of men, among whom the greatest number of suicides occur in the early to middle adult years (25–54) and the greatest rates occur in the older adult years (>65). . . .

One demographic variable that is not often considered is geographic location. Suicide rates vary considerably by region. For example, Alaska had the highest rate of female suicides in 2000, and the District of Columbia had the lowest. . . .

Regional variability may reflect a variety of factors, including risks associated with the age of the population, the ethnic or racial cohorts of the region, access to and availability of mental health treatment, and access to and familiarity with firearms.

Marriage is often reported as a protection against suicide, with a particularly strong effect for men. The strength of marriage as a protective factor in women is less robust, but is suggested by multiple studies. There are many limitations in our understanding of this demographic factor. Few have delineated marital status into a continuum of categories (never married, widowed, divorced, separated, married), and even fewer have noted living arrangements or partnered (heterosexual or same sex) relationships. . . .

How Are Women Different?

Current data provide some insight into areas for investigation and highlight similarities and differences in men and women that may allow for the development of sex- or age-specific prevention initiatives. . . .

The most robust and compelling finding for men and women who commit suicide is the high prevalence of psychiatric illness. All major affective, psychotic, anxiety, and substance abuse disorders have been shown to increase the risk of suicide. One obvious paradox exists, however. Major depression, which has repeatedly been found to be a significant risk factor for suicide, affects women in the early and middle years of life at twice the rate of men, yet women die by suicide at one-quarter the rate of men. In later life, the rates of depression may be roughly equal, but the suicide rate in men skyrockets while the rate in women drops. These data argue that major depression alone is insufficient to account for suicide and does not explain sex differences in suicide rates.

Depression is highly prevalent among women who die by suicide. The prevalence of depressive disorders in selected studies from European and Asian countries is between 59% and 91%, with similarly high rates in the United States. One investigative team concluded that the prevalence of depression was greater among women who committed suicide than in the general population. . . .

Among women who die by suicide, alcohol abuse is also highly prevalent. In the 5 studies that reported alcohol or other substance abuse, between 59% and 17% of women met study criteria. . . .

Pregnancy and Parenthood Are Protective

Being pregnant and having young children in the home have each been found to have a protective effect against maternal suicide. The duration of the protective effect of parenthood is unknown and is not absolute. For example, investigators found an increased risk among parents who experienced the death of a child or whose child had a psychiatric illness. Another exception is in the case of postpartum psychiatric illness, which is associated with an increased suicide risk. Some studies also suggest a higher rate of suicide among women who have undergone induced abortions. . . .

Education and Employment Affect Suicide Risk for Women

Specific types of employment may confer greater suicide risk. Data from death certificates of adult female suicides between 1975 and 1979 from 4 states revealed that suicide rates were greatest among the "moderately traditional" job holders, followed by "nontraditional" jobs, and finally those in "highly traditional" jobs. . . .

Using the National Mortality Followback Survey, researchers found that women who died by suicide were more likely to have higher levels of education than women who died from natural causes. This finding is consistent with studies in which higher rates of suicide among women physicians were found when compared with women in the general population or women working in other professions. Women physicians in Finland had a standardized mortality ratio of 2.4 and 3.7 between 1986 and 1993 when compared with women in the general population and women professionals respectively. Similarly, increased rates of suicide have been found among US women physicians. . . .

Other professions that have elevated rates of female suicide include police officers (4 times the general population rate) and Navy personnel (1.3 times the civilian rate). All of these may be considered "nontraditional" professions for women, and all have potentially contributing factors, such as access to and familiarity with lethal means. Further studies are required to understand the individual characteristics of women involved in these professions as well as the social and cultural stressors associated with performing these jobs.

How Do Women Kill Themselves?

It is often noted that women choose "less lethal means" (e.g., overdose, wrist cutting) than men do. Many consider the choice of means to be responsible, in part, for the distribution of female and male suicides and suicide attempts. With this in

Breast Implants Linked to Suicide Risk

Women who receive implants for breast enhancement are three times more likely to commit suicide, according to a new report that offered a sobering view of an increasingly popular surgery.

Deaths related to mental disorders, including alcohol or drug dependence, also were three times higher among women who had the cosmetic procedure, researchers said.

The report in the Annals of Plastic Surgery's August issue was the most recent to detect a higher suicide rate among women who had their breasts enlarged, providing a gloomy counterpoint to studies that showed women felt better about themselves after getting implants.

Though the study did not look at the reasons behind the suicides, senior author Joseph McLaughlin, a professor of medicine at the Vanderbilt University School of Medicine, said he believed that many had psychological problems before getting implants and that their conditions did not improve afterward.

Denise Gellene, "Breast Implants Linked to Suicide Risk,"
Los Angeles Times, *August 8, 2007.*

mind, it often surprises clinicians that, for more than a decade, firearms have been the most common method of suicide among women. In 2000, firearms accounted for 37% of female suicides, followed by overdose (31%), hanging (17%), and all other forms (15%). The use of firearms is not limited to young women; there was a 46% increase in the use of firearms (24% to 35%) among older women who died by suicide between 1980 and 1992. Increasing familiarity with and access to firearms are the hypothesized causes of the increase. Access to firearms increases the odds of suicide for both sexes.

Comparing Male and Female Suicides

A substantial body of literature exists about factors that may protect women against suicide. Interpretation of these factors derives primarily from considering why men die of suicide more often than women do. One explanation is that women use less lethal means than men do. A study comparing 61 female suicides with 143 male suicides found that 43% of the women used "more immediately fatal means" (defined as firearms, hanging, jumping) compared with 75% of men. It is well-established that women attempt suicide with nonlethal means more often than men do, however, it is also true that when suicide attempts are defined as serious (i.e., requiring medical attention), the incidence among men and women is equal. Because of the sex distribution of suicide attempts and deaths, the literature is heavily skewed toward risk factors for suicide attempts among women and, conversely, risk factors for suicide deaths among men. From the current literature we cannot know whether suicide attempters are inherently different from completers or not. However, these 2 groups overlap with regard to common psychiatric disorders.

A second prominent theory is that women's "social embeddedness" is protective. Parenthood can be protective, although its protective value is not absolute and must be considered in the context of other factors. It has also been hypothesized that women are at greater risk of suicide when they deviate from traditional roles. Declining rates of suicide among women as they increasingly enter traditional male professions fail to support this notion, but it is true that there is a higher rate of suicide among certain, nontraditional professions.

Finally, because women use mental health services more than men do, it would follow that women are more likely to be treated for depression or other contributing psychiatric illnesses and therefore would be at lower risk of suicide. This hypothesis does not explain the high rates of suicide attempts among women, however, nor can it be the only explanation, as more than half of women with depression remain undiagnosed or un- or undertreated.

Identifying and Helping Woman at Risk of Suicide

How can physicians identify the woman at risk of suicide? Physicians can use the information gained at a population level to guide and enhance their assessment of an individual woman. The available data highlight the need to ask about psychopathology, including symptoms of depression or bipolar disorder; alcohol and substance abuse; previous psychiatric history, including inpatient hospitalizations and suicide attempts, delusions, history of violence, impulsivity, or aggressive behavior. Physicians also should ask about a woman's access to and familiarity with firearms; her relationships, including marital, parental, and reproductive status; her children's health status; her family history of suicide; her level of education; her age; and her profession. No suicide scale exists to total these risk factors and decide a woman's overall risk, but inquiring systematically about these factors provides physicians an avenue to explore the woman's state of mind. At the same time, it is an opening to direct inquiry about key components of any suicide assessment.

> "Something about modern life is killing more and more young men by suicide, but at the same time is not affecting young women."

Men Are Particularly at Risk for Suicide

Ciaran Mulholland

In the following viewpoint, Ciaran Mulholland asserts that the suicide rate for men worldwide is rising. Mulholland discusses the signs, symptoms, and treatments of depression, which is a primary risk factor for suicide. Although more women suffer from depression, more men take it to its ultimate and devastating outcome: suicide. Mulholland says that although the reasons are not precisely clear, the rising suicide rate for men is definitely related to their changing role in society. Ciaran Mulholland is a psychiatrist and lecturer in mental health at Queens University in Belfast, Northern Ireland.

As you read, consider the following questions:

1. According to Mulholland, what is the lifetime rate of depression for men? For women?

Ciaran Mulholland, "Depression and Suicide in Men," *Netdoctor.co.uk*. April 1, 2005. Reproduced by permission. Available at http://www.netdoctor.co.uk/menshealth/facts/depressionsuicide.htm.

2. Mulholland says that being male is a risk factor for suicide. Name three other suicide risk factors he describes.

3. According to Mulholland, what percentage of those who attempt suicide actually complete suicide?

What Is Depression?

Depression is often used in everyday language to mean straightforward and understandable unhappiness. This use of the term is best avoided. Instead, the word should be reserved for those who have significant and pervasive lowering of mood leading to difficulties in leading a normal life. Such conditions can vary from a lifelong predisposition to low mood (known as dysthymia) to depressive episodes that vary in intensity from relatively mild to severe.

Depression is likely to be one of the greatest, if not the greatest, disease burdens of the 21st century. It is a very common condition that causes a great deal of suffering and a substantial number of deaths. Depression leads to disharmony at home, difficulties at work and internal distress. Unfortunately, the condition still attracts much stigma, is not always recognised and, when recognised, is not always adequately treated. Depression is more common in women than in men, though its most dramatic outcome, death by suicide, is more common in men.

How Is Depression Diagnosed?

The diagnosis of depression is made when several core features are present:

- pervasive low mood

- loss of interest and enjoyment (anhedonia)

- reduced energy and diminished activity.

Other features can also be present, including:

- poor concentration and attention

- poor self-esteem or self-confidence

- ideas of guilt and unworthiness

- a bleak pessimistic view of the future

- thinking about, planning, or attempting suicide

- crying for no reason

- disturbed sleep

- poor appetite

- decreased interest in sex.

Depression is often more difficult to diagnose in men because they do not complain of these typical symptoms so often. They are less likely to admit to distress, and if they do consult their doctor, tend to focus on physical complaints.

How Common Is Depression?

In community surveys, 2 per cent of the population suffer from pure depression at any one time. Some have a mild form of the illness, some moderate and some severe, in roughly equal numbers. Another 8 per cent of the population suffer from a mixture of anxiety and depression at any one time. Other people do not have symptoms severe enough to qualify for a diagnosis of either anxiety or depression but have impaired working and social lives and unexplained physical symptoms.

The lifetime rate of depression is 8 per cent for men and 12 per cent for women, and these figures seem to be rising. This trend is worrying and has been much discussed. Depression is now more frequently diagnosed in younger people than it was previously. This change could well be a result of the increasing social fragmentation, including family break-down, seen over recent decades.

How Is Depression Treated?

Mild episodes of depression often get better without treatment or will respond to simple measures such as changes in the social environment or the family situation. Many other patients can be treated adequately by their [General Practitioner] GP. Only a minority of patients ought to be referred to specialist psychiatric services.

Patients who should be referred include those:

- who are thought to have a high risk of committing suicide

- who fail to respond to the usual treatments

- in whom the diagnosis is confusing or difficult to make.

If depression co-exists with other conditions that complicate treatment, such as a physical illness, patients should usually be referred to a specialist. Patients with a psychotic depression, who are troubled by delusions (abnormal beliefs) or hallucinations, should always be referred.

Surveys clearly show that patients prefer a psychotherapeutic approach (counselling or talking about their problems) or at least expect such an approach in combination with their medication. Evidence indicates that certain specific forms of psychotherapy are useful for patients with mild, moderate and severe depression. Their usefulness is most obvious in the milder forms and in the prevention of further episodes of depression. Men are less likely to ask for this form of treatment.

Since the late 1950s, effective medication has been available for depressive illness. In recent years, new antidepressants, with fewer side effects, have become available. These are effective for most people and relatively easy to tolerate. Whichever antidepressant is used, it is important to continue treatment for six to nine months after symptoms resolve otherwise symptoms might return quickly. Antidepressants are equally effective in men and women. . . .

Patients with psychotic depression are seriously ill and will almost always require hospitalisation. Antidepressant therapy alone is unlikely to be effective. The treatments of choice are either electroconvulsive therapy (a highly effective but controversial treatment that involves passing electricity through the brain under general anaesthetic) or a combination of an antidepressant with an antipsychotic medicine (a type of medication that treats delusions and hallucinations).

Suicide and Men

Suicide accounts for 1 in 100 deaths but the majority of those are men. A worrying recent trend is the increasing rate of suicide among younger men (a trend not seen among young women). The majority of these men have not asked for help before their deaths. The suicide rate in men also increases in those aged between 65 and 75 years. In contrast, the suicide rate in women varies less with age.

The higher suicide rate among men is a worldwide phenomenon. A few exceptions to the general rule exist, for example, among elderly women in Hungary and in some Asian countries. The reasons why men are more likely to kill themselves than women are complex and ill-understood. However, several pointers help our understanding.

As well as being male, several other risk factors for suicide have been identified.

- **Age:** suicide in men peaks in the 20s and again in the 60s and 70s.

- **Unemployment:** the suicide rate has been shown to rise and fall with the unemployment rate in a number of countries—half of the record 33,000 people who committed suicide in Japan in 1999 were unemployed.

- **Social isolation**: those who kill themselves often live alone and have little contact with others; they may have been recently widowed or have never married.

- **Chronic illness**: any chronic illness increases the risk of suicide.

- **Certain occupations**: people with certain occupations are more likely to die by suicide, for example, farmers (who usually work alone, may be unmarried and have access to the means of suicide, such as a shotgun or poisonous weedkiller).

Many of the above risk factors affect men more than women. It is important to remember that many people are subject to these factors, but only a tiny minority of them will end their own lives.

Other factors are also significant. The most important risk factor is the presence of a mental illness. The most important protective factor is the presence of good support from family or friends.

Mental Illness

Research has shown that the vast majority of those who kill themselves are mentally ill at the time of their death. Two thirds are troubled by a depressive illness and 20 per cent by alcoholism.

Of people with severe depressive illnesses, 10–15 per cent will commit suicide. Paradoxically, as mentioned above, depressive illnesses are more common in women, but suicide is more common in men. Several possible explanations exist for this apparent discrepancy.

The more severe the depression is, the more likely it is to lead to suicide. So one possibility is that more severe forms of depressive illness are equally common in men and women. In addition, once men are depressed, they are more likely to end their lives. They are also more likely to choose especially lethal methods when they attempt suicide, for example, hanging or shooting. Depressive illness among people under 25 years of age is probably much more common now than it was 50 years ago, which may account for one reason why the suicide rate is increasing in young men.

Alcoholism leads to suicide in 10 per cent of affected people. Alcoholism is much more common in men (though it is increasing rapidly among women).

Schizophrenia (a relatively uncommon condition affecting 1 in 100 of the population) leads to suicide in 10 per cent of affected people.

Why Is the Male Suicide Rate Rising?

The reasons why the number of men taking their own lives has risen in recent years are far from clear. All of the proposed explanations share a common feature—the changing role of men in society.

Adolescence has been prolonged, with adulthood and independence reached at a much later age than previously. Two generations ago, work began at the age of 14; one generation ago at 16 years for most; now many men only achieve financial independence in their 20s.

Men have a more stressful time in achieving educational goals than in the past and are now less successful than women.

Work is much less secure and periods of unemployment are the norm for many (psychologically the threat of unemployment is at least as harmful as unemployment itself).

Alcohol use, and abuse, has increased markedly since the Second World War. Such use is often an attempt to cope with stress and to self-medicate symptoms.

Illegal drug abuse has become much more common (a correlation between the youth suicide rate and the rate of convictions for drug offences has been demonstrated in some countries).

Changes that are assumed to be symptoms of the 'breakdown of society' are associated with a rising suicide rate (examples include the rising divorce rate and falling church attendances).

Boys Don't Cry

In many societies, expressing emotions, for example sadness, fear, disappointment or regret, is seen as being less acceptable for boys than girls.

This cultural stereotype is very, very difficult to shake off, though the advent of 'new men' in the 1990s has made it more acceptable for men to open up to others.

If a man, particularly an older man, does cry openly, this is often a sign of severe depression and is taken very seriously indeed by health professionals.

Deliberate Self-harm

Some of those who 'attempt' suicide do not actually intend to kill themselves. They mimic the act of suicide by taking an overdose or cutting themselves. They do so in an attempt to change an intolerable situation or gain attention from significant other people in their lives. This process is know as deliberate self-harm or parasuicide. Such people can get considerable relief of tension and anxiety from these acts. Deliberate self-harm is more common in women, though the proportion of men who self-harm is increasing.

Some 10–15 per cent of those who attempt suicide go on to complete suicide. In other words, 85–90 per cent do not. . . .

Barriers to Effective Treatment of Depression in Men

- Men are less likely to recognise that they are under stress or unhappy, let alone ill.

- Men are less likely to consult their doctor when distressed.

Wrestler's Suicide Calls Attention to Alarming Trend

Suicide is identified as [a] rising global problem primarily affecting men. Know its risk factors and how can it be prevented.

The suicide of [World Wrestling Entertainment] WWE wrestler Chris Benoit again called the attention of the public to an alarming trend that certainly needs to be addressed. While not uncommon; there are other prominent wrestlers like Michael Lee Alfonso (popularly known as Mike Awesome) and "Bam Bam" Bigelow who have committed suicide and succeeded.

With an investigation going on, Benoit's suicide is largely attributed to steroid and illicit drug use and emotional stress similar to those cases mentioned above. However, Benoit's suicide is just the tip of the iceberg to what is really a global problem primarily affecting men's health.

Sam Bag-ao, "Suicide Among Men,"
Menshealth.suite101.com, *July 3, 2007.*

- If they do consult their doctor, they are more likely to complain of physical symptoms (for example, stomachache) or vague ill-health.

- Health professionals are often less likely to consider a diagnosis of mental illness in men.

- Some of the young men who kill themselves without ever seeking help seem to not have an identifiable mental illness. Rather, they are troubled by a philosophical dilemma, a dis-ease (sic) of the soul, for which suicide seems the solution.

What Can Society Do?

Something about modern life is killing more and more young men by suicide, but at the same time is not affecting young women. We need to know more about why this is happening and if necessary society must consider changes in the way we live to reduce the toll of suicide.

- About 80 per cent of women who have committed suicide will have consulted their doctors and received treatment before their deaths.

- Only 50 per cent of men will have done so.

- For men aged less than 25 years of age, the proportion is only 20 per cent.

Education campaigns might help men, and young men in particular, to seek assistance rather than suffer in silence.

> *"Notwithstanding such wild exaggerations, there is no consensus among experts that anything resembling an 'epidemic' of gay teen suicides exists."*

Homosexuality Does Not Increase Risk of Suicide for Teens

Peter LaBarbera

In the following viewpoint, Peter LaBarbera argues that the gay teen suicide epidemic is a myth perpetuated by homosexual activists and based on faulty research. LaBarbera says that many of the statistics used to support the claim that gay teens are at an increased risk of suicide are from a flawed report written by homosexual activist Paul Gibson. LaBarbera says that activists are using the erroneous statistics to push for pro-gay programs in schools. Peter LaBarbera is the president of Americans for Truth, an organization that seeks to counter the homosexual activist agenda.

As you read, consider the following questions:

1. According to LaBarbera, what did David Shaffer say about Gibson's paper?

Peter LaBarbera, "The Gay Youth Suicide Myth," *Insight*, February, 1994. Reproduced by permission of Family Research Council, 801 G Street, NW, Washington, DC 20001, 1-800-225-4008, www.frc.org. Available at http://www.leaderu.com/jhs/labarbera.html.

2. Name three of what LaBarbera describes as Gibson's most tendentious and oft-repeated claims.

3. According to LaBarbera, programs like Project 10 encourage impressionable teens to do what?

The rate of suicide has nearly tripled among young people since 1965. Efforts to discover the root causes of this epidemic of self-inflicted violence must be dispassionate and free of politics. However, homosexual activists have manipulated this national tragedy to promote their political agenda.

Voicing concern over suicide risk for "gay youth," homosexual activists are pushing pro-homosexual programs in the schools, which will invariably ensnare vulnerable teens who might otherwise have avoided the destructive homosexual lifestyle. Their diagnosis: gay youths need affirmation of their homosexuality in a "homophobic" world, or they may become suicidal. The proffered solution: affirmation programs that make gay youths comfortable with being homosexual and the rest of the student population comfortable with the concept of homosexuality. Once everyone accepts homosexuality as "normal" and "natural," gay youth will achieve high self-esteem and avoid suicidal behavior.

But this view is based on the aims and values of the gay activist movement, not on any solid scientific assessment. For starters, it ignores the possibility that homosexuality is a condition—apart from societal acceptance or nonacceptance—that often leads to unhealthy behavior, which leads to unhappiness.

Flawed Report Perpetuates Gay Teen Suicide Myth

The genesis of the homosexual teen suicide myth lies in a deeply flawed and pro-homosexual report by San Francisco homosexual activist Paul Gibson. The paper, "Gay Male and Lesbian Youth Suicide," was included, as a supporting document, in a 1989 report by a special federal task force on youth suicide reporting to Dr. Louis Sullivan, former Secretary of Health and Human Services (HHS). However, Secretary Sullivan repudiated and distanced his department from the Gibson paper:

> ... the views expressed in the paper entitled 'Gay Male and Lesbian Youth Suicide' do not in any way represent my personal beliefs or the policy of this Department.

Sullivan went on to say:

> Indeed, I am strongly committed to advancing traditional family values. Federal policies must be crafted with great care so as to strengthen rather than undermine the institution of the family. In my opinion, the views expressed in the paper run contrary to that aim.

Dr. David Shaffer, one of the country's leading authorities on suicide among youth, notes that Gibson's paper "was never subjected to the rigorous peer review that is required for publication in a scientific journal and contained no new research findings."

The following are some of Gibson's most tendentious and oft-repeated claims:

- gay and lesbian youths may account for one third of all youth suicides;

- homosexual youths are two to three times more likely to attempt suicide than their heterosexual peers;

- suicide is the leading cause of death among gay and lesbian youth; and

- gay youth suicide is caused by the internalization of "homophobia" and violence directed at gays.

Although Gibson's report was denounced by Secretary Sullivan, homosexual activists have skillfully used it to claim that "government statistics" support their suicide assertions. Pro-gay articles routinely (and mistakenly) cite Gibson's unproven statistics as part of the HHS task force's official conclusions on youth suicide. Gibson himself has declined an interview with the author to discuss his controversial assertion.

Suicide "Scare" Being Used to Push Gay Agenda in Schools

In Massachusetts, a recently established Commission on Gay and Lesbian Youth set up by Republican Gov. William Weld relied almost exclusively on Gibson's unpublished HHS paper to warn ominously of a gay teen suicide epidemic. Gibson's exaggerated claims became the central rationale for creating a sweeping pro-gay counseling program in the state's schools. In an interview in *The Advocate*, a national gay magazine, Governor Weld, curiously, uses a Gibson-derived statistic to justify the program while at the same time seemingly acknowledging that this program may have credibility problems: "They say the harassment is one of the reasons gays and lesbians account for 30% of teenage suicides. That doesn't even need to be true for me to say that fighting anti-gay discrimination in the schools is absolutely necessary."

Lobbying by public school students was the key to passage of a student "gay rights" bill in Massachusetts, and, again, Gibson's "30 percent" statistic was a factor. According to *The New York Times*, a student stood outside the State House for several weeks leading up to the December 6, 1993 Senate passage of the bill holding a sign that said "Gays Make Up 30 Percent of Completed Teen Suicides." David LaFontaine, a gay activist who is now the director of Weld's youth commission, went so far as to say, "Gay youth suicide is like a hidden holocaust in America."

Notwithstanding such wild exaggerations, there is no consensus among experts that anything resembling an "epidemic" of gay teen suicides even exists. Moreover, many observers are

In short, while [Paul] Gibson's non-facts are still being used by homosexuals to promote the recruitment and seduction of children in our nation's public schools, there is now new evidence from Cornell's [Ritch] Savin-Williams, showing that suicide among homosexual teens is no more likely than among heterosexual teenagers.

The cold, hard fact is that teens who are struggling with homosexual feelings are more likely to be sexually molested by a homosexual school counselor or teacher than to commit suicide over their feelings of despair.

Traditional Values Coalition
"Homosexual Urban Legends 30% of Teen Suicide
Victims Are Homosexuals," Traditional Values Coalition.

aghast that, in this age of AIDS, the danger of suicide would be used to confirm confused youths in an unhealthy, destructive lifestyle that is fraught with anxiety and disease and that often leads to early death.

Due in large part to the effective use of the suicide scare, Massachusetts teenagers in public schools are now facing an array of pro-gay counseling programs similar to Project 10—the Los Angeles school program set up by a lesbian teacher with the goal of "validating the feelings" of "lesbian and gay youth." Project 10's blatant pro-gay bias is exemplified by its name, which is based on the now-repudiated myth that homosexuals make up 10 percent of the population. . . .

Some Teens May Be Confused About Their Sexuality

There appears to be evidence that youth confused about their sexuality are at greater risk for suicide. But it is foolhardy to use the polemical work of Paul Gibson as proof that there is an "epidemic" (or worse, a "holocaust") of gay youth suicides that requires drastic action. Homosexual activists who do so risk expanding the cracks in their already fractured credibility.

Further research and careful debate on this issue are warranted. Ann Garland of the Department of Psychology at Yale University wrote recently, "There is considerable debate over whether homosexuality is a risk factor for suicide." There is also great disagreement among psychiatrists over whether suicide intervention programs in schools actually work; some believe they cause more harm by *implanting* the idea of suicide in the minds of impetuous youth. Shaffer, Garland, and other specialists on suicide write that "to date there is no evidence of even marginal efficacy" of school-based suicide intervention programs.

Dangers of Pro-Homosexual Counseling

Although the increase in general youth suicides in recent years certainly warrants concern, Shaffer notes that "suicide is a relatively uncommon cause of death; fewer than 20 boys out of every 100,000 who are alive, will commit suicide in a year." Great care must be taken not to endanger youths who otherwise would not be touched by suicide in the name of "rescuing" a tiny portion of the teen population who, in reality, are not best or most accurately identified by their struggles over sexuality.

Moreover, Gibson himself cites Remafedi in noting that the "earlier a youth is aware of a gay or lesbian orientation, the greater the problems they face and more likely the risk of suicidal feelings and behavior." Paradoxically, programs like Project 10 *encourage* impressionable teens to take that potentially lethal step of "identifying" themselves as homosexuals at a young age.

The dangers of pro-homosexual counseling programs of the type envisioned by homosexual activists to "rescue" suicidal "gay and lesbian teens" is perhaps best described by former homosexual Alan Medinger:

> In schools all over the country, children . . . are being labeled "sexual minority" students and are being led to counselors drawn from the gay community. How often are the deeply rooted needs and biases of these "counselors" going to lead them to counsel the "unsure" that they are gay? "Unsure" in their minds often means that the youngster is simply afraid of coming to terms with his or her homosexuality . . .

From every medical and health aspect—up to and including the probability of becoming infected with AIDS—it is tragic, even criminal to lead a child into homosexuality because he or she showed some degree of sexual confusion in adolescence.

> "Elderly people have a higher risk of completed suicide than any other age group worldwide. Despite this, suicide in elderly people receives relatively little attention."

The Elderly Are Most at Risk for Suicide

Henry O'Connell, Ai-Vyrn Chin, Conal Cunningham, and Brian A. Lawlor

In the following viewpoint, O'Connell, Chin, Cunningham, and Lawlor maintain that the phenomenon of elderly suicide draws sparse attention, in spite of the fact that more elderly people complete suicides than any other age group. The authors dispel the myth that suicidal thoughts are a natural part of the aging process. Rather, they say that elderly suicides are usually caused by a complex interplay between psychological factors—with depression being the most prominent—physical factors and social factors. They offer some treatment and prevention measures and say that elderly suicides should receive more attention from researchers. Henry O'Connell and Ai-Vyrn Chin are research asso-

Henry O'Connell, Ai-Vyrn Chin, Conal Cunningham, Brian A. Lawlor, "Recent Developments: Suicide in Older People," *BMJ*, vol. 329, October 16, 2004, pp. 895–899.

ciates; Conal Cunningham is a research consultant; and Brian Lawlor is a professor of psychiatry at Mercer's Institute for Research on Ageing, Dublin, Republic of Ireland.

As you read, consider the following questions:

1. According to a comprehensive review of psychological autopsy studies, 71–95 percent of elderly people who committed suicide had what?

2. The authors categorize elderly people as being "young old" or "old old" What age separates the young old group from the old old group?

3. When discussing the impact social factors may have on elderly suicides, the authors compare the pre-suicide stressful life events that elderly people tend to face with those that younger people seem to face. Describe the stressful life events that elderly people seem to experience before suicide. List four stressful life events typically associated with suicide in younger populations.

Elderly people have a higher risk of completed suicide than any other age group worldwide. Despite this, suicide in elderly people receives relatively little attention with public health measures, medical research, and media attention focusing on younger age groups. We outline the epidemiology and causal factors associated with suicidal behaviour in elderly people and summarise the current measures for prevention and management of this neglected phenomenon. . . .

Dispelling the Myths (Greek and Otherwise)

From time immemorial, suicidal feelings and hopelessness have been considered part of ageing and understandable in the context of being elderly and having physical disabilities. The Ancient Greeks tolerated these attitudes in the extreme and gave elderly people the option of assisted suicide if they could plead convincingly that they had no useful role in society. Such practices were based on the assumption that once an individual had reached a certain age then they no longer had any meaningful purpose in life and would be better off dead. Although not as extreme, ageist beliefs in modern, especially industrialised, societies are based on similar assumptions. Sigmund Freud echoed such views, while suffering from incurable cancer of the palate:

> It may be that the gods are merciful when they make our lives more unpleasant as we grow old. In the end, death seems less intolerable than the many burdens we have to bear.

The burden of suicide is often calculated in economic terms and, specifically, loss of productivity. Despite lower rates of completed suicide in younger age groups, the absolute number of younger people dying as a result of suicide is higher than that for older people because of the current demographic structure of many societies. Younger people are also more likely to be in employment. Therefore the economic cost of suicide in younger people is more readily apparent than that in older people.

The burden of suicide should not, however, be measured solely in such reductionist terms, and the extent of the real burden on families and communities from suicide in elderly people cannot be overemphasised. Furthermore, the ageing of populations worldwide means that the absolute number of suicides in elderly people is likely to increase.

Epidemiology of Suicidal Behaviors

One model of the suicidal process is that suicidality exists along a continuum. Following this model, the epidemiology of suicidal behaviours in elderly people can be described broadly under the headings of suicidal ideation, attempted suicide, and completed suicide.

The prevalence of hopelessness or suicidal ideation in elderly people varies from 0.7–1.2% up to 17% in different studies, depending on the strictness of criteria used. A universal finding is the strong association with psychiatric illness, particularly depression. The prevalence of suicidal feelings in mentally healthy elderly people has been reported to be as low as 4%. These findings are therefore contrary to the ageist assumption that hopelessness and suicidality are natural and understandable consequences of the ageing process.

Rates of completed suicide in elderly people vary between cultures, but pooled international data published by the World Health Organization show a steady rise in prevalence of completed suicide with age. For men, the rate increases from 19.2 per 100,000 in the 15–24 year old age group to 55.7 per 100,000 in the over 75s. For women, the respective rates are 5.6 per 100,000 and 18.8 per 100,000. The male to female ratio for completed suicide in the elderly is 3 or 4:1, similar to that of other age groups.

Although the prevalence for completed suicide in elderly people does not at first suggest a major public health problem, completed suicides are likely to represent only the tip of the iceberg for psychological, physical, and social health problems in older people.

According to a comprehensive review of psychological autopsy studies, 71–95% of elderly people who completed suicide had a psychiatric illness, most commonly depression. Major depressive disorder has been found to be more common in completed suicides among older people than among younger counterparts and may affect as many as 83% of elderly people who die as a result of suicide. The prevalence of completed suicide is, however, relatively low among elderly people with primary psychotic illness, personality disorders, anxiety disorders, and alcohol and other substance use disorders.

Data for suicidal behaviours, especially attempted suicide, between elderly and younger people suggests that different phenomena are involved.

The ratio of parasuicides [i.e. an apparent suicide but where the aim is not death] to completed suicides in elderly people is much lower than that among younger people and among the general population (200:1 in adolescents. 8:1–33:1 for the general population, and 4:1 in elderly people). Suicidal behaviour among elderly people is therefore more likely to carry a higher degree of intent. This is further supported by the reported increased use of lethal means by older people, such as firearms and hanging.

Factors Associated with Suicide in Elderly People: Re-examining the Files of Usual Suspects

A wide variety of factors have been implicated in suicidal behaviour in elderly people. These can be described broadly as psychological, physical, and social factors. Such factors are either modifiable, such as physical and psychiatric illness, or non-modifiable, such as sex and social class. A description of modifiable and non-modifiable factors may provide insights into factors associated with suicidal behaviour in elderly people.

The case-control study, using psychological autopsies (information gathered after death from relatives, healthcare professionals, and medical records), is the most commonly used method for examining risk factors and associations for suicide in older people. Recent research has also focused on differences in risk factors for suicide between "young old" (under 75 years) and "old old" populations. The importance of such research is reflected in the epidemiology of suicide in elderly people, in view of the increased risk for those aged over 75 years.

Psychological Factors

According to psychological autopsy studies of suicides in elderly people, 71–95% of the people had a major psychiatric disorder at the time of death. Depressive illnesses are by far the most common and important diagnoses. In the only prospective, non-clinical cohort study of older people to date in which completed suicide was the outcome, self rated severity of depressive symptoms was the strongest predictor of suicide. Those people in the poorest summary score category were 23 times more likely to die as a result of suicide than those with the least depressive symptoms. Other important psychological factors included drinking more than three units of alcohol a day and sleeping nine or more hours at night. The generalisability of these results is limited, however, because the people were living in a retirement community. A recently published retrospective case-control study found that alcohol use disorders predicted suicide in older people. A history of alcohol dependence or misuse was found in 35% of elderly men and 18% of elderly women who had died as a result of suicide, with corresponding rates in controls of only 2% and 1%.

A review summarised the findings of four psychological autopsy studies that examined the effect of psychiatric illness on completed suicide. Any axis I psychiatric disorder was associated with a substantially increased risk of completed suicide, with odds ratios ranging from 27.4 to 113.1. One of the studies found an odds ratio of 162.4 for recurrent major depressive disorder, with single episode major depression, dysthymia, and minor depression being important but less powerful predictors of completed suicide. Older people with psychotic depression may have a still further increased risk of completed suicide, although a recent study found no difference in the numbers of suicide attempts between psychotic and non-psychotic depressed elderly inpatients.

Other psychiatric illnesses, such as anxiety disorders, psychotic disorders, and substance use disorders, have also been implicated as risk factors for suicide in elderly people, but seem to be significantly less important than depressive illnesses.

Although three of the four studies that examined dementia diagnoses found no significant difference between people who died as a result of suicide and controls, more detailed examination of the nature and anatomical location of cerebrovascular disease is likely to provide clinically useful information in the future. Traditionally, an increased risk of suicide in patients after stroke was thought to be secondary to depression and functional impairment. However, strategic infarcts specifically affecting frontal and subcortical circuitry have been associated with both depression and impulsivity, and the importance of cerebrovascular disease in suicidal thoughts and behaviour in older people has been argued. In addition, a case-control study found that Alzheimer's disease was over-represented at autopsy in elderly people who had died as a result of suicide.

In keeping with findings in younger populations, significantly lower concentrations of 5-hydroxyindoleacetic acid and homovanillic acid have been found in the cerebrospinal fluid of elderly people who died as a result of suicide compared with non-suicidal and normal controls.

The roles of personality type and traits have been studied in elderly people who died as a result of suicide. Clinical experience suggests that the effects of ageing on the brain, physical health problems, and life events such as bereavement may coarsen or accentuate pre-existing maladaptive personality traits in certain elderly people and make them more likely to engage in suicidal thinking or behaviour.

Elderly people who die as a result of suicide have been shown to have higher levels of neuroticism and lower scores for openness to experience, having a restricted range of interests and a comfort with the familiar. Interestingly, the only controlled study assessing personality disorder diagnosis, found that it was not over-represented in elderly people who died as a result of suicide.

Model of Suicidality

Feelings of hopelessness and despair

    Thoughts that life is not worth living

    Passive wish to die

    Suicidal ideation

    Suicide plans

    Suicide attempts

    Completed suicide

Henry O'Connell et al.,
"Recent Developments: Suicide in Older People,"
British Journal of Medicine, *October 16, 2004.*

A follow up study of 100 elderly people who had attempted suicide two to five years after the index attempt found that 42 had died, 12 being suspected suicides and five dying as a delayed result of the index attempt. Twelve women had attempted a further non-lethal attempt and five men had completed suicide after a further attempt. Recent case-control studies identified a history of a suicide attempt as a risk factor for suicide in older people. These studies highlight the importance of secondary prevention strategies targeted at those who have attempted suicide.

Physical Factors

Although problems with physical health and level of functioning are important in the cause of suicidal behaviours, controlled studies suggest that their effects are generally mediated by mental health factors, most notably depression. A recent psychological autopsy study of completed suicide in nursing home residents highlighted the complex interplay between physical and psychological factors.

Having more than three physical illnesses and a history of peptic ulcer disease in a population sample of community dwelling residents aged over 85 years were predictive of increased suicidal feelings. Physical health and disability seem to be associated independently of depression with the "wish to die." This death wish was also found to be associated with the highest comorbidity in a large sample of older patients attending their general practitioner for depression, anxiety, and at risk alcohol use.

Based on a review of 235 prospective studies, physical disorders were associated with an increased risk of suicide, including HIV/AIDS, Huntington's disease, multiple sclerosis, peptic ulcer, renal disease, spinal cord injury, and systemic lupus erythematosus. A retrospective case-control study, however, found that neither current serious physical illness nor a visit by a general practitioner in the previous month was significantly associated with completed suicide. Two other retrospective case-control studies found the burden of physical illness and current serious physical illness to be significantly associated with completed suicide in elderly people. Depression was not accounted for in the first of these studies, however, and when included in the analysis in the second study, the effects of physical illness became non-significant. A retrospective case-control study did find that serious physical illnesses (visual impairment, neurological disorders, and malignant disease) were independent risk factors for suicide. The authors concluded that serious physical illness may be a stronger risk factor for suicide in men than in women, implying that elderly males may be more vulnerable to the effects of physical health problems. These findings have important implications for the detection and management of suicide in elderly people, highlighting the importance of psychiatric evaluation in people with physical disorders.

There are also important ethical implications; the fact that there is a high prevalence of potentially treatable psychiatric illness in those elderly people who have both physical illness and suicidal ideation should be central in any discussion on physician assisted suicide.

Social Factors

As with other age groups, elderly people seem to have an excess of stressful life events in the weeks before suicide. The nature of these may differ in older people, with more emphasis on physical illness and losses, such as bereavement, and less emphasis on interpersonal discord, financial and job problems, and legal difficulties; these last four factors are more typically associated with suicide in younger populations. Some recent studies have, however, found an association between interpersonal discord and suicide, even in later life.

Decreased social support and social isolation are generally associated with increased suicidal feelings in elderly people. An influential study suggested that elderly people who had died as a result of suicide were more likely to have lived alone. More recent studies do not agree with these findings, but they did report that loneliness and low social interaction were predictive of suicide.

Religiosity and life satisfaction were found to independent protective factors against suicidal ideation in elderly African-Americans. Similar findings have been reported in terminally ill elderly people, where higher spiritual wellbeing and life satisfaction independently predicted lower suicidal feelings.

In general, widowed, single, and divorced elderly people have a higher risk of suicide, with marriage seeming to be protective. Bereavement is also associated with attempted and completed suicide in elderly people—men seem especially vulnerable after the loss of a spouse, with a relative risk three times that of married men. In contrast, widowed and married elderly women seem to have a similar risk. A recent study concluded that the protective effect of marriage was not apparent in those aged over 80 years, showing how risk factors for suicide may differ between young old and old old.

Although several social factors associated with suicide in elderly people are non-modifiable, they may give clues as to the underlying biological processes involved in suicidal ideation and behaviour. For example, the increased vulnerability of elderly men to bereavement and physical illness may be mediated by relatively higher levels of cerebrovascular disease and alcohol use disorders compared with elderly women.

Detection

Despite the higher risk of completed suicide in elderly people compared with younger age groups, the low absolute prevalence rate does not justify screening of the entire elderly population. Screening for suicidal ideation should be opportunistic, with high risk subgroups defined and targeted, based on knowledge of psychological, physical, and social factors. High risk subgroups include those with depressive illnesses, previous suicide attempts, or physical illnesses, and those who are socially isolated. Elderly people with multiple such factors warrant special attention.

Older people are less likely to volunteer that they are experiencing suicidal feelings. Moreover, these feelings may be present in patients with few depressive symptoms, and feelings might not be manifest unless asked about directly. Healthcare professionals should be trained and encouraged to ask such questions directly. The presence of suicidal feelings in depressed patients also predicts a lower response to treatment and an increased need for augmentation strategies, thereby identifying a group of patients who may need secondary referral.

Management

The estimated population attributable risk for mood disorder in elderly suicide is 74%. This means that if mood disorders were eliminated from the population, 74% of suicides would be prevented in elderly people. "Elimination" of mood disorders is achieved not only by treatment of existing cases but also by the prevention of new cases and secondary prevention of subclinical cases. The level of detection and treatment of depression of all ages in the general population is low, and only 52% of cases that reach medical attention respond to treatment. Detection rates and treatment response are likely to be still lower in elderly people. Thus, although treatment of depression is vital in combating suicide in elderly people, preventive measures at an individual and population level are also essential. Improved physical and emotional health, exercise, and modification of lifestyle should promote successful ageing and lead to a decrease in the incidence of suicidal feelings.

Interventions at population level that improve social contact, support, and integration in the community are also likely to be effective, especially considering that the population attributable risk factor for low social contact is 27%. For example, telephone help lines have been associated with a significant reduction in completed suicide in elderly people.

Limiting access to the means of suicide (for example, over the counter medicines) or decreasing the chance of completed suicide (for example, reducing the lethality of car exhaust fumes with catalytic converters) have been shown to have benefits for the general population and are also likely to affect suicide rates in elderly people, particularly considering the increased use of lethal means by older people.

An appropriate strategy for the prevention of suicide might be the introduction of opportunistic screening for hopelessness and suicidal feelings in elderly people who visit their general practitioner. This is especially important because of the high level of contact found between elderly people and their general practitioner in the week before suicide (20–50% contact) and in the month before suicide (40–70% contact). [A recent] study highlighted the importance of training for general practitioners to lower the incidence of suicide in all age groups. Such training is also likely to lead to improved detection and management of elderly people with suicidal tendencies. A study of depression in primary care highlighted the importance of increasing doctors' awareness of depression and suicide in elderly patients. Compared with young adults with depression, old old (over 75 years) patients were only 6% its likely to be asked about suicide, one fifth as likely to be asked if they felt depressed, and one fourth as likely to be referred to a mental health specialist.

Conclusion

Suicide in elderly people is a complex and multifactorial phenomenon. Elderly people are frequently sidelined in discussions on suicide, perhaps as a result of factors such as a higher overall number and a higher economic burden associated with suicide in younger people and ageist beliefs about the elderly and ageing in modern, particularly industrialised, societies.

Screening, prevention, and management programmes should focus more on elderly people, in view of the inherent increased risk of suicide in this population. More specifically, there is a need for vigorous screening and aggressive treatment of depression and suicidal feelings in elderly people, especially in subgroups with additional risk factors such as those with comorbid physical illness and those who are socially isolated.

Periodical Bibliography

The following articles have been selected to supplement the diverse views presented in this chapter.

Jane E. Brody

"A Common Casualty of Old Age: The Will to Live," *New York Times.* November 27, 2007.

Laura Fitzpatrick

"The Gender Conundrum," *Time.* November 19, 2007.

Harvard Health Publications Group

"Youth Suicides Jump, Especially for Girls," *Harvard Reviews of Health News.* September 10, 2007.

Timothy F. Kirn

"Suicide Rate Among Army Personnel Climbs to 26-Year High," *Family Practice News.* September 15, 2007.

Diana Mahoney

"Suicide Rates Spike in Youth and Young Adults," *Clinical Psychiatry News.* October, 2007.

Julie Mehta

"When Life Hurts: Some Teens Are in so Much Emotional Pain, They Think Life Is Unbearable, But There Is Help—and Hope," *Current Health.* December 2006.

Tim Murphy

"Stormy Weather: This Fall the CDC Reported the Greatest Spike in the Number of Teen Suicides in 15 Years. What Does This Mean for Gay Youths?" *The Advocate.* October 23, 2007.

E.M. Swift

"What Went Wrong in Winthrop? One High School Football Team, Five Suicides in Three Years. Can We Learn Anything?" *Sports Illustrated.* January 9, 2006.

Michelle Tan

"Desperate Housewives: Women on the Verge," *People Weekly.* September 17, 2007.

Mitchel L. Zoler

"Clue into Suicide Risk Among Elderly Patients," *Family Practice News.* November 1, 2007.

OPPOSING
VIEWPOINTS®
SERIES

CHAPTER 2

What Are Some of the Causes of Suicide?

Chapter Preface

"On the edge of the edge, lonely Jimmy Getal has the weight of the world on his shoulders. After a failed suicide and at the end of his rope, Jimmy, a superintendent at one of old Hollywood's 'has-been' and 'neverwere' apartment complexes forces himself to go to work one more day. However, today will include a life or death ultimatum to test his own fate. If at the end of the day he has more negative experiences than positive ones, Jimmy will jump off the rooftop to his death." This is the synopsis of an indie film released in 2000 called *Between Christmas and New Years*. Included with the synopsis on the film's Web site at www.filmbaby.com are several statistics about suicide including the following: There is an increase of suicides between Christmas and New Year's Day in the United States.

Many Americans mistakenly believe that suicides increase during the holidays, particularly Christmas. However, mental health experts say that suicides do not increase around Christmas and that this is a myth perpetuated by the media.

The Christmas holiday can cause many people to experience the "blues." Christmastime is *supposed* to be a time of happiness and cheer. At least that's what the media displays: Families getting together, gifts overflowing under the Christmas tree, and beautiful homes decked out in Christmas decorations. However, many people do not experience Christmas this way. Many people are far away from their loved ones, cannot afford holiday gifts, and don't have beautiful homes. Additionally, family get-togethers can be filled with tension. People whose Christmas realities do not meet expectations can suffer the holiday blues. Headaches, excessive drinking, overeating, and difficulty sleeping are some symptoms of the holiday blues. However, statistics show that people who experience the blues around the holidays do not usually attempt suicide.

Mental health experts say that suicide actually decreases in the winter around Christmas, when compared to other times of the year. "The general belief is that the holidays are actually characterized by greater cohesion and emotional support rather than conflict, and the extra support makes a difference," says David Rudd, chairman of the Department of Psychology at Texas Tech University. As psychologist John McIntosh explains further, "when the weather is cold we spend more time inside around other people. So, there are more people to hear our problems, to share with, and just to be with. So we're more likely to recognize pain and depression and either give help or get help for that person."

Statistics show that suicides are actually at their highest in the spring and the summer. McIntosh thinks the most important reason that suicides increase in spring and summer is unmet expectations. Says McIntosh, "specifically, we associate spring and, to a lesser extent, summer with new beginnings and life. People who are depressed may well make it through the bleak winter by looking forward to that new beginning. However, when they reach that expected point, that is spring, their life doesn't change positively the way they may have expected. The disparity of those expectations with reality may be the proverbial straw that broke the camel's back. This person in great psychological pain may now feel he or she can no longer tolerate that pain. So suicide is increased."

The media perpetuates the myth that suicides increase at Christmas. Since 1999, the Annenberg Public Policy Center (APPC) of the University of Pennsylvania has been tracking how the media reports about suicides around the holidays. A typical media story might begin talking about the holiday blues and then incorrectly attribute the arrival of the holiday season with an uptick in suicides. The APPC found that about 77 percent of articles written about suicide during the Christmas and New Year's holidays in 1999–2000 perpetuated the myth. The APPC has tried to educate the media and make the public aware that suicides do not increase at Christmastime, and it appears they have had some impact. In 2005–2006, only about 57 percent of suicide stories incorrectly linked suicide with the holidays, while 43 percent attempted to dispel the myth. "We are heartened to see the press debunking the myth," said Kathleen Hall Jamieson, director of the APPC, "but there is still a lot of coverage that keeps the story alive." Mental health experts are concerned that continuing the holiday suicide myth can be detrimental to those who need help. "Perpetuating the myth not only misinforms readers, but it also misses an opportunity to educate the public about the most likely source of suicide risk, mental illness," according to Dan Romer, director of the APPC's Adolescent Risk Communication Institute. Romer believes the press can help those suffering from mental illness by reporting accurately about the holidays and suicide.

Statistics show that the holiday blues do not necessarily cause people to commit suicide. So what are the causes of this harrowing act? The contributors of the viewpoints in the following chapter explore some of the complex reasons people take their own lives.

| *"Complete strangers may make cyber-space pacts."*

Suicide Internet Sites Can Cause Suicide

Sundararajan Rajagopal

In the following viewpoint, Sundararajan Rajagopal explores the many facets of suicide pacts and identifies Internet Web sites as a potential growing problem. Rajagopal advises that while the percentage of suicides involving suicide pacts is small, health-care practitioners should remain watchful of this emerging trend. Sundararajan Rajagopal is a consultant general adult psychiatrist at St Thomas' Hospital in London, England. Dr. Rajagopal's special interests include the placebo effect, "cybersuicide", suicide pacts, systematic reviews, and teaching.

As you read, consider the following questions:

1. According to Rajagopal, why are the 2004 suicide deaths of nine people in Japan significant?
2. According to Rajagopal, what percentage of the total number of suicides involve suicide pacts?
3. What is "cybersuicide"?

The recent deaths of nine people in Japan, in October 2004, apparently in two suicide pacts—seven suicides in one pact and two in the other—have brought the relatively rare phenomenon of suicide pacts into the limelight. What is unusual is that these pacts seem to have been arranged between strangers who met over the internet and planned the tragedy via special suicide websites. This is in contrast to traditional suicide pacts, in which the victims are people with close relationships.

What Is a Suicide Pact?

A suicide pact is an agreement between two or more people to commit suicide together at a given place and time. In England and Wales, for epidemiological purposes, people who have committed suicide within three days of each other in the same registration subdistrict are considered potential victims of a suicide pact. A related phenomenon is homicide-suicide, in which a person commits a murder and then ends his or her own life. Dyadic death is a term that encompasses both suicide pacts and homicide-suicides. A suicide cluster is a group of suicides that occur closer together in time and space than would normally be expected in a given community, with suicides occurring later in the cluster being motivated by earlier suicides. In mass suicide, several people commit suicide usually influenced by charismatic leadership, strong loyalties, or religious beliefs.

Two major epidemiological studies on suicide pacts have been carried out in England and Wales, 36 years apart. The second study showed that the incidence of suicide pacts had declined by 27% in that period. On average, one suicide pact occurs every month. Suicide pacts almost always involve people well known to each other, mostly spouses, most of them childless. Most of the victims belong to social classes I, II, and III [lower-to-middle class], and a noteworthy proportion work in professions allied to medicine. The methods used are generally less violent; poisoning by exhaust fumes from a vehicle is the most common. But where access to violent means is easier, such as firearms in the United States, suicide pacts entail more violent methods. Most victims leave jointly signed suicide notes.

Although, by definition, both victims make a joint decision to die in a suicide pact, studies of survivors of pacts have shown that this is not always the case. In cases where the decision was not mutual, the deceased member is likely to have been the instigator, male, depressed, and to have had a history of self harm, whereas the survivor is likely to be the coerced, female, not mentally ill, and with no previous history of self harm.

Percentage of Suicide Pacts Is Small

Suicide pacts account for less than 1% of the total number of suicides. Both members typically employ the same method. Occasionally, the partners may both use multiple methods to ensure death. About half have psychiatric disorders and a third have physical illnesses. In an international comparison of suicide pacts, pacts between spouses were found to predominate in the United States and England, between lovers in Japan, and between friends in India. The relationship between victims of suicide pacts is typically exclusive, isolated from others, and the immediate trigger for the pact is usually a threat to the continuation of the relationship, for example, impending death of one member from an untreatable physical illness.

Suicide pacts have been associated with a rare psychiatric disorder called *folie á deux*. In this condition, two people share the same or similar delusional beliefs. The relationship among people with this psychotic disorder is also usually enmeshed and isolated from the rest of society. Just as in some suicide pacts where one person instigates the plan, in *folie á deux* the delusion is characteristically imposed by the dominant mem-

alt.suicide.holiday Web Site

The alt.suicide.holiday [a.s.h.] Usenet newsgroup features discussions about life, depression and suicide. However, a.s.h is special in that suicide is legitimate both as a desire and an action. Suicide is not encouraged but is also not denounced.

a.s.h is not a support group in the normal sense, but paradoxically it gives many readers strength to carry on.

What is ash? What is it about? What is it good for? Part 1 of the ASH FAQ, answers these questions and provides an introduction to the community. We also explain what ash is not.

Part 2 of the FAQ describes the way ashers talk and behave online, whereas Part 3 offers an explanation to those who question whether ash is genuine.

alt.suicide.holiday, Introduction. Available at http://ashbusstop.org/ash.html. August 27, 2007.

ber of the relationship on to the other person. While suicide pacts are usually seen between spouses, *folie á deux* is commoner among sisters, usually spinsters.

Internet Plays a Role

The potential negative role of the internet in relation to suicides has been highlighted previously. An increasing number of websites graphically describe suicide methods, including details of doses of medication that would be fatal in overdose. Such websites can perhaps trigger suicidal behaviour in predisposed individuals, particularly adolescents. Cybersuicide refers to suicides or suicide attempts influenced by the internet. Scientific literature on cybersuicide mainly pertains to solitary suicides, and little information exists about the internet and suicide pacts.

The recent suicide pacts in Japan might just be isolated events in a country that has even previously been shown to have the highest rate of suicide pacts. Alternatively, they might herald a new disturbing trend in suicide pacts, with more such incidents, involving strangers meeting over the internet, becoming increasingly common. If the latter is the case then the epidemiology of suicide pacts is likely to change, with more young people living on their own, who may have otherwise committed suicide alone, joining with like minded suicidal persons to die together.

General practitioners and psychiatrists should continue to remain vigilant against the small but not insignificant risk of suicide pacts, especially while encountering middle aged depressed men who have dependent submissive partners. While assessing risk, one may specifically ask whether a depressed patient uses the internet to obtain information about suicide.

> "Spectacular media reports of suicides following Internet contact and case reports of individuals who died by suicide using methods they found on the Internet or in pacts with people they met over the Internet, as impressive as they may seem, do not constitute scientific proof that Internet activities provoke suicides."

Suicide Internet Sites Should Not Be Censored

Brian L. Mishara and David N. Weisstub

In the following viewpoint, Brian Mishara and David Weisstub argue against censoring Internet sites that promote suicide. They contend that there are numerous legal, ethical, and practical issues that make regulating suicide Web sites extremely difficult. Furthermore, the authors claim that there just isn't enough valid scientific data to prove that suicide Web sites actually cause suicides. They suggest alternatives to censorship. Brian Mishara is the director of the Center for Research and Intervention on Sui-

Brian L. Mishara and David N. Weisstub, "Ethical, Legal, and Practical Issues in the Control and Regulation of Suicide Over the Internet," *Suicide and Life-Threatening Behavior*, vol. 37, February, 2007, p. 58–65. Copyright © 2007 The American Association of Suicidology. Reproduced by permission.

cide and Euthanasia, and David Weisstub is a professor of legal psychiatry and biomedical ethics at the University of Montreal, Canada.

As you read, consider the following questions:

1. According to Mishara and Weisstub, meeting suicide companions online seems to be most prevalent in what country?
2. According to Mishara and Weisstub, what technology has been characterized as a "pull technology?" What are two examples of "push technologies?" Compare and contrast the characteristics of pull technologies and push technologies.
3. What is the only country according to the authors, that has laws to specifically restrict Internet sites that promote suicide?

There has been growing concern about the numerous reports of suicides following contact with Web sites that incite people to suicide and provide detailed information on suicide methods. The ethical, legal, and practical issues in the control and regulation of suicide promotion and assistance over the Internet are the focus of this article.

Media Coverage of "Online" Suicides

There are numerous reports in the media and scientific journals of suicides purportedly related to contact with Internet sites. Typical examples include the suicide that instigated the introduction of a bill in the Danish Parliament in February 2004 to ban Web sites that encourage and provide information about suicide. The son of a Danish journalist was apparently encouraged to end his life by a Web site which gave him information he used to kill himself. Two studies that reported on a 17-year-old female suicide attempter concluded that Web sites may trigger suicidal behavior in predisposed adolescents.

Several newspaper articles tell of distraught parents who blamed their child's suicide on Internet sites, and there was much media coverage of a 21-year-old man from Arizona who killed himself by overdose while chatting online with friends who egged him on.

Multiple suicides by people who meet on chat sites appear to be increasing. One much-publicized example concerned Louis Gillies from Glasgow who met Michael Gooden from East Sussex (England) in May 2002 on a suicide "newsgroup". While on a cliff ready to jump, Gillies was talked out of killing himself by a friend on his cell phone, but Gooden refused to talk and jumped. Gillies was charged with aiding and abetting a suicide; he killed himself in April 2003 just before the trial was about to begin.

Meeting suicide companions online appears to be most prevalent in Japan where, between February and early June 2003, at least 20 Japanese died in suicide pacts with companions they met on the Internet, many by strikingly similar carbon monoxide poisonings. . . . It is believed that the first "wave" of Internet suicide pacts occurred in 2000 in South Korea when there were three cases. In March 2003, an Austrian teenager and a 40-year-old Italian who met on a suicide chat jointly committed suicide near Vienna. The man had also contacted two young Germans online, but police alerted their families before they could carry out their suicides.

Anti-Suicide Laws Not Applied to Internet

Many countries have laws prohibiting aiding and abetting suicide; however, we are not aware of any case where Internet activity has been pursued in a court of law for aiding or abetting suicide. That said, on February 13, 2005, Gerald Krein was arrested in Oregon for solicitation to commit murder after it was alleged that he used his Internet chat room to entice up to 31 lonely single women to kill themselves on Valentine's Day. The arrest followed a report to police by a woman in the chat room who said another participant talked about killing her two children before taking her own life.

So why have not current laws against aiding and abetting suicide been applied to Internet activities, given the compelling nature of specific case histories when people died by suicide in a manner communicated over the Internet and following a series of Internet contacts in which they were aged to kill themselves? It may be helpful to examine legal jurisprudence regarding standards for determining causality in such matters. When individuals are deemed to be responsible for having caused harm to another person, their actions are usually in close temporal and physical proximity to the victim's death. For example, a person who strikes another person who subsequently dies from the blow may be deemed responsible because that action had an immediate physical consequence for the victim. In addition, scientific and medical evidence must indicate according to reasonable probabilities that the action in question was causally related to the consequences.

Influencing Is Not the Same as Causing

Scientific research on the influence of the media on suicides has concentrated on television and newspapers and their influence on population suicide rates. There are several excellent reviews of research in this area. It is clear that news media depictions of deaths by suicide have a risk of increasing suicides among those who have contact with those media. Generally, the more the publicity, the higher the contagion effect (it has been reported that the suicide of Marilyn Monroe resulted in 197 additional suicides), however, there are no empirical data on changes in the risk of suicide that may be related to contacts with Internet sites. Nevertheless, it appears from numerous cases reported in the media that contact with Internet sites and with chat rooms preceded deaths by suicide and the methods used were precisely those described in the Internet contact. In sum, these case reports do not meet the requirements for scientific proof that Internet sites cause suicide, but they suggest that a relationship may exist.

Despite the compelling case reports, it can be argued that had the victims not contacted a specific suicide site, they may have still killed themselves. The suicide risk of people who contact suicide sites may have pre-dated their contact. In addition, if a person had not used a method found on a site, other methods are easily available.

Another challenge in determining a causal relationship is the difficulty in generalizing from epidemiological population statistics to individual cases. . . .

The nature of epidemiological research is such that, given the great number of people at risk of committing suicide and the very small number who actually die by suicide, it is impossible to determine that one specific individual is likely to have died as a result of media exposure and that the death could have been avoided by non-exposure.

To date we do not have any epidemiological data on the relationship between contact with the Internet and suicides. All we have is a number of case histories in which there appears to be a link. It is dubious that one could make a good scientific or legal case for the causal relationship between Internet activities and suicide without conducting further research.

Protecting Freedom of Expression

Even if one could prove that there is a risk associated with certain Internet sites, one must weigh that risk against possible dangers of compromising freedom of expression by attempting to control access to the site. In most countries, there is little or no control of Internet content because of constitutional guarantees of freedom of expression. . . .

Many countries, including Great Britain, Canada, the United States, and New-Zealand, attempt to control Internet content by self-regulation since guarantees of freedom of speech apparently preclude censorship or government control of access to sites. . . .

A number of countries attempt to block access by all individuals to specific Internet content and sites, including Algeria, [Bahrain], China, Germany, Iran, North Korea, Saudi Arabia, Singapore, South Korea, Sweden, United Arab Emirates, and Vietnam. For example, in Saudi Arabia all 30 of the ISPs go through a central node, and material and sites containing pornography, believed to cause religious offense, and information on bomb making are blocked. . . .

In several countries, including the United States, Great Britain, and New Zealand, laws were passed to block certain Internet content, but those laws were overturned by the courts because of constitutional guarantees of freedom of expression. Australia is the only country that currently has laws to specifically restrict sites that promote suicide or provide information on suicide methods. . . .

Ethical Questions

There are several ethical considerations concerning the control of Internet content in order to prevent suicide. First and foremost is the ethical premise that suicide should be prevented. Those who adopt a libertarian perspective might contend that people have the right to choose to end their life by suicide. Also, since suicide is not illegal in most countries, one could argue that suicidal people should have access to material they desire. If this libertarian position is adopted, it is not possible to justify controlling access to information encouraging suicide or providing information or advice on how to exercise the right to end one's life by suicide.

If one adopts a moralist ethical position that suicide must be prevented, and if controlling access to Internet sites can save lives, then controls must be instituted. If one holds a relativist position that some suicides are acceptable and others are not, one may morally justify some form of Internet control, although control of access for only some people is practically impossible. For example, a relativist who believes that terminally ill people should be allowed or have access to means to end their lives but people in good health who suffer from treatable psychiatric problems should not, would have a difficult time controlling access for some people and not others.

Internet Is Different from TV and Radio

One of the questions concerning the ethics of controlling access to the Internet is the specificity of the Internet compared to other mass media. The Internet has been characterized as a "pull" technology, as opposed to the so-called push technologies including radio and television. Push technologies include television and radio; they provide access to the media without the user engaging in any specific and explicit attempt to find a specific media content. Television content is available in every home and because of its universal access, television has been regulated in most countries as to content. In contrast to the mass medias of television and radio, Internet users must actively seek out a specific content.

Also, anonymity of the provider can exist on the Internet and there is no ability to verify the authenticity of the information one finds on a Web site. No government agencies are ensuring that Web content is appropriate and accurate (unlike television and radio which are generally subject to government control). The Web can be extremely graphic in nature and individuals who display their suicidal intentions and behaviors on the Internet can expect possible exposure to thousands throughout the world, providing glorification of their suicidal acts.

The differences between "push" and "pull" technologies may be used to defend the Internet against control by claiming that the Internet is a private service that does not invade people's homes, and that specific content must be sought out by individuals actively searching through cyberspace. The down side, of course, is this same private nature provides for a level of anonymity of both the person contacting the site and the person providing information on a site, which may lead to an "anything goes" environment where there are no controls whatsoever about the authenticity and credibility of information transmitted or provided.

Which Activities to Ban?

Internet situations involving suicide vary. Some sites passively provide information, which encourage suicide in texts that suggest it is a good idea to end one's life. Other sites provide information on suicide methods, many including specific details about what medications to mix, how to hang oneself, and the strengths and weaknesses of alternative methods with respect to side effects and risks of failure. Yet still other sites involve the exchange of messages from "suicide encouragers" who interact with suicidal people, trying to stimulate them to proceed with their suicidal plans in chat rooms or in e-mail correspondence. "Suicide predators" seek out people who post messages suggesting they may be feeling suicidal but who are not explicitly asking for information or encouragement. These predators offer unsolicited incitation to suicide and may provide information about how to commit suicide without being asked. If one is considering some form of control of Internet activity, it is important to decide which of the above activities one would like to limit.

Protecting Vulnerable Populations

One of the major issues in control of the Internet in order to prevent suicides is the protection of minors and other vulnerable populations, such as persons with psychiatric disorders. The most successful attempts to control access over the Internet has involved child pornography sites and pornography aimed at minors, although these initiatives may be criticized for falling short of their goal of totally blocking access. Thus far, very little has been done to protect minors from suicide promotion sites. . . .

Jurisdictional Challenges

Even if one were able to resolve the legal and ethical issues, there are a number of practical considerations that make control of Internet suicide promotion activities extremely difficult. The first is the issue of cross-border jurisdiction. Although countries may be able to control activities of Internet sites that originate within their borders, international jurisprudence makes it difficult to obtain jurisdiction over sites that originate outside the country. Jurisprudence generally distinguishes between passive Internet activity, such as simply operating a Web site which may be accessed from different countries, and active endeavors which involve sending information, interacting (for example, in a chat room), and doing business in a country. Furthermore, jurisprudence has favored limiting claims of harm to actual impact rather than claims of potential damage. . . .

More Data Needed

There remains a great need for scientifically valid data on the extent that Internet sites contribute to the risk of suicide. Specifically, we need to determine if Internet activities increase suicide risk and, if so, which subpopulations are particularly vulnerable. Spectacular media reports of suicides following Internet contact and case reports of individuals who died by suicide using methods they found on the Internet or in pacts with people they met over the Internet, as impressive as they may seem, do not constitute scientific proof that Internet activities provoke suicides. One could try to build a case for the relationship between Internet activities and suicide using psychological autopsy methods. Qualitative assessments of the content of Internet contacts where seemingly vulnerable individuals appeared to be forcefully encouraged to kill themselves has high face validity; however, we need to develop more creative methodologies, perhaps inspired by the studies of the relationship between suicide reporting in other media and sui-

Why Suicide Sites Should Not Be Banned

[Louis] Gillies was accused of making a pact with Michael Gooden via a website called Alternative Suicide Holidays. According to the Guardian newspaper the site has been "frozen". It . . . describes itself as a "partial sanctuary where people can discuss suicide openly in an atmosphere which is not condemnatory of suicide, as much of 'western' culture is". The site insists it does not encourage suicide, but does not dissuade people either.

Suicide websites have long been the subject of criticism. Many people argue that they can push people over the edge when they are depressed and should therefore be banned. Some people attempt a more "politically correct" view and argue that suicide sites should be forced to present the opposing view with links to the Samaritans [A suicide prevention website]. If, like most people, you are generally opposed to the idea of people taking their own lives, it can seem hard to avoid reaching either of these conclusions.

However, there is something very important at stake here and that is the ability of people to make up their own minds about things. Certainly some people are mentally ill and cannot be trusted to make their own judgements in general. Shutting down websites is a poor substitute for the sort of medical assistance that this kind of illness requires. For the rest of us, even depression does not mean we should be deprived of the right to form our own opinions. Once we allow certain ideas to be suppressed for "our own protection", we all lose a fundamental democratic freedom. Worse still, we all end up being treated as if we were mentally ill.

Chris Evans, "Why Suicide Sites Should Not Be Banned,"
Internetfreedom. *Available at* www.netfreedom.org. *July 14, 2003.*

cide rates. One of the greatest challenges is to determine if individuals who kill themselves after Internet contacts would have died by suicide if they did [not] use the Internet.

It is also important to clarify the ethical basis upon which any form of suicide prevention activity is undertaken before applying one's beliefs to controlling Internet suicide promotion. Furthermore, any action to control Internet suicide promotion must consider the different forms of Internet activities, which range from passive posting of information on a Web site to interacting in a chat room or seeking out vulnerable individuals as an Internet predator.

Censorship Is Dangerous

Any attempt to control the Internet must be viewed along with the control and freedom of other media, unless special characteristics of the Internet are judged to lead to special laws or consideration. It can be argued that, unlike other media, the internet lacks quality control, and this may justify legislative intervention. Most keep in mind, however, that editors of newspapers, like Web masters, are free to publish what they please, even if it may incite suicides. If a journalist publishes a "dangerous" article, she may evoke the ire of readers and sales may decline (or increase due to the controversy). When a Web site or chat does something people do not like, users can simply not frequent that site. In this regard it is interesting to compare the Internet to published works. If one were to publish the philosopher David Hume's writings recommending suicide on an Australian Internet site, would this be banned? If so, would it be considered as more dangerous than publishing his book and selling it in a bookstore? Internet sites provide information on means to kill oneself in an often clear but informal manner; however, if the same information is available in medical textbooks, what would justify control of this information over the Internet while permitting the sale of medical textbooks and their availability in libraries?

Alternatives to Censorship

The fact that the Internet allows for global access leads to complex jurisdiction issues and practical difficulties. Given the rapidly changing state of technologies which lead to the continued development of new ways to circumvent control, it may not be practically possible to ban sites, censor material, or limit access. Even if data to document that high risks of suicide are related to specific Internet activities were available, and even if a country decides to prevent access to suicide sites, the only way to ensure even a minimal level of success would be to install draconian censorship measures. Regardless, it is not certain that the controls would be effective. Therefore, alternatives to control and censorship should be considered, such as developing increased suicide prevention activities on the Internet to counterbalance Internet suicide promotion activities. Persons involved in suicide prevention should be encouraged to enter chat discussions to dissuade suicidal persons from killing themselves and encourage them to seek help. Finally, public education could be enhanced to facilitate ways and means to obtain help from the Internet in the interest of suicide prevention.

> "In 2000, the FDA stated that there were 147 known suicides linked to Accutane."

Accutane Causes Suicide

Kevin Caruso

In the following viewpoint, Kevin Caruso implores people not to use the anti-acne medication, Accutane. Caruso says there is overwhelming evidence that shows the medication is linked to depression, aggressive behavior, suicidal thoughts, and suicides. According to Caruso, the manufacturer of Accutane has not been forthcoming to the Food and Drug Administration (FDA), the agency responsible for ensuring drug safety in the United States, about the adverse side effects of the medication. Kevin Caruso is the founder and executive director of www.suicide.org, a suicide prevention Web site.

As you read, consider the following questions:

1. What was the name of the public interest group that petitioned the FDA to ban Accutane?

2. According to Caruso, an FDA memo indicated that there were a number of Accutane-related abortions by 1990. How many abortions did the memo link to Accutane?

3. According to Caruso, in 2000, the FDA linked how many known suicides to Accutane?

There are many reasons why you and your loved ones should not use Accutane; but the most important reason is this: It can cause you to die by suicide.

So, DO NOT use Accutane, under any circumstances, and DO NOT allow your loved ones to use Accutane.

Period.

There are innumerable SAFE alternatives to Accuatane, so you and your loved ones do not need to use it. Ever.

The Facts about Accutane

Now, let's examine some important facts about Accutane.

The drug was introduced in 1982 and is manufactured by Roche. It is a strong acne medication and is supposed to be used for severe acne as a "treatment of last resort." But many dermatologists prescribe Accutane for mild or moderate cases of acne without even trying an alternative treatment first.

Accutane can cause severe, and even tragic, side effects and psychiatric problems, including birth defects, miscarriage, fetal death, Crohn's disease, central nervous system injuries, cardiovascular injuries, bone and muscle loss, ulcerative colitis, pancreatitis, immune system disorder, depression, and suicide.

In September 1983, Public Citizen, a national non-profit public interest organization, petitioned the [U.S. Food and Drug Administration] FDA for warning labels because of the high risk of these side effects.

In 1986, Roche changed Accutane's package insert to indicate that some users reported symptoms of depression.

In 1988, Public Citizen petitioned the FDA for a ban on Accutane.

By 1990, an FDA memo indicated that there had been 11,000 to 13,000 Accutane related abortions and 900 to 1,100 Accutane related birth defects.

In 1996, an FDA document indicated that more than 90 percent of females who were prescribed the drug did not have severe acne.

Worries from the French

In 1997, French health authorities required Roche to add a warning to their package insert indicating the possibility of suicide to the list of Accutane's possible side effects; but Roche did not inform the FDA about this action.

A few months later, the FDA issued a stern warning letter to Roche for failing to submit serious adverse event reports; unbelievably, Roche STILL had not informed the FDA about the French mandated warning about Accutane being a possible cause for suicide.

In 1997, A Roche doctor [studied] data on depression in Accutane patients, leading him to recommend users be supervised for signs of depression and, if necessary, referred for treatment.

In February 1998, the FDA concluded that Roche had not acted in good faith and recommended "active consideration of removal of Accutane from the market."

They also advised doctors who prescribed Accutane to closely monitor their patients for signs of depression, and they required bold face warnings to physician package inserts which stated the following: "Psychiatric disorders: Accutane may cause depression, psychosis and, rarely, suicidal ideation, suicide attempts and suicide. Discontinuation of Accutane therapy may be insufficient; further evaluation may be necessary. No mechanism of action has been established for these events."

FDA Requires Accutane Maker to Warn Doctors

Below is the entire "Dear Doctor" letter that the FDA required Roche to distribute to all doctors who prescribed Accutane:

February 1998

Dear Doctor:

Please be advised of important changes to the prescribing information for Accutane (isotretinoin).

The information pertaining to Adverse Experience reports of depression, which has appeared in the ADVERSE REAC-TIONS section of the prescribing information, will now also appear in the WARNINGS section. The following revisions will be made:

- the WARNINGS section will now begin with the following paragraph in bold type:

- "Psychiatric disorders: Accutane may cause depression, psychosis and, rarely, suicidal ideation, suicide attempts and suicide. Discontinuation of Accutane therapy may be insufficient; further evaluation may be necessary. No mechanism of action has been established for these events."

- the paragraph on depression in the ADVERSE REACTIONS section will become paragraph 5 of that section and will be revised as follows:

- "In the post-marketing period, a number of patients treated with Accutane have reported depression, psychosis and, rarely, suicide ideation, suicide attempts and suicide. Of the patients reporting depression, some reported that the depression subsided with discontinuation of therapy and recurred with reinstitution of therapy."

It is important to note that reports of these Adverse Experiences are uncommon but, because of their potential consequences, clinicians should be attentive to any new behavioral signs and symptoms. . . .

FDA "Talk Paper" about Accutane

Below is the FDA "Talk Paper" which was released in association with the February 1998 warnings about Accutane. Note that a "Talk Paper" is distributed by the FDA to its own personnel so that they will be prepared to respond with "consistency and accuracy" to questions from the public.

February 25, 1998

IMPORTANT NEW SAFETY INFORMATION ABOUT ACCUTANE

FDA today is advising consumers and health care providers of new safety information regarding the prescription anti-acne drug Accutane (isotretinoin) and isolated reports of depression, psychosis and rarely suicidal thoughts and actions.

Accutane was approved in 1982 to treat only a very special type of acne—severe nodular acne that has not responded to other therapies.

> Although the Accutane label already included information regarding depression as a possible adverse reaction, the agency felt health care providers and others needed additional information as a result of adverse event reports the agency has received.

FDA and the drug manufacturer are strengthening this label warning, even though it is difficult to identify the exact cause of these problems. Such problems could already be more common among the patient populations likely to be on the drug.

However, because some patients who reported depression also reported that the depression subsided when they stopped taking the drug and came back when they resumed taking it, the agency and the manufacturer felt the strengthened labeling was warranted as a precautionary measure.

Given the complex nature of depression and suicidal conditions, the new label information will advise health care providers that merely discontinuing the drug may be insufficient to remedy these adverse events, and that further evaluation may be needed. . . .

Suicide Victim Hoped to Play in a Band

[Liam] Grant, one of four siblings, was an engineering student at University College Dublin. His father says Liam played guitar and drums in bands and hoped to launch a career recording music.

Medical records show that Liam did not suffer from the severe, treatment-resistant acne for which Accutane is prescribed. Dr. Pamela Mangal prescribed an antibiotic, then wrote a stronger prescription in December when Liam was unhappy with the results. One month later, she referred him to Dr. Gillian Murphy, a dermatologist, who prescribed Roaccutane, the drug's market name in Ireland. Liam started taking it in February 1997.

His father says he should have noticed the potential warning signs that ensued. Liam, previously outgoing and enthusiastic about his plans, increasingly spent time alone in his bedroom. When friends called, he asked one of his brothers to tell them he was unavailable.

In June 1997, Liam was found dead, hanging from a tree outside Dublin. A jury, impaneled to investigate the case, ruled the death a suicide and called for more research on Accutane and its side effects.

Kevin McCoy, "Grieving Father Spends 1 million Nest Egg to Investigate Accutane," USA Today. January 26, 2006.

Mounting Complaints

In March 1998, Health officials in Britain and Ireland require warnings of Accutane's risk of psychiatric disorders.

In 1999, Roche responded to mounting complaints about Accutane causing suicidal thoughts and suicide by adamantly telling the FDA that none of the 168 reports of suicidal behavior could be linked to Accutane.

In 2000, the FDA stated that them were 147 known suicides linked to Accutane.

In 2000, Roche changed Accutane's package warning label to include possible side effects involving depression, rare suicidal thoughts, suicide attempts, and suicide.

In May 2000, Bart Stupak, Jr., son of Congressman Bart Stupak, died by suicide by shooting himself in the head. Representative Stupak would later say that Accutane was the cause for his 17-year-old son's suicide.

Stupak said that the Accutane package did not include any warnings about the possibility of depression or suicide and that the doctor did not tell them about the possibility either.

The congressman and his wife, Laurie, said they considered every possible cause for their son's suicide and "the only thing we can find is Accutane."

In 2002, the FDA informed a congressional committee that the agency had received reports of 3,104 adverse psychiatric events and 173 suicides associated with Accutane.

In 2002, the Accutane label is changed to warn of "depression, psychosis and, rarely, suicidal ideation, suicide attempts, suicide, and aggressive and/or violent behaviors."

In November 2004, FDA researcher David Graham testified before Congress that Accutane should be carefully scrutinized to determine whether the drug should continue to be on the market in the United States. Graham describes Accutane as "a 20-year regulatory failure by the FDA."

In December 2004, USA Today stated that Roche ignored an internal doctor's recommendation that people who take Accutane be monitored for signs of depression and that a warning be placed on the drug's U.S. label stating this.

Accutane Affects Brain Function

In 2005, a study was published in the *American Journal of Psychiatry* concerning the effects of Accutane.

The study began by conducting brain scans on 28 acne sufferers. Next, the 28 subjects underwent psychological tests to ensure that they were not depressed.

Then, the patients received either Accutane or an antibiotic for four months.

Afterwards, the subjects underwent a second brain scan which was then compared to their original scan.

The results of the study clearly indicated that the Accutane patients had decreased activity in the area of the brain associated with mood regulation.

"What we can say is that Accutane affects brain function . . . and the areas that are affected are the areas involved with depression," said Dr. J. Douglas Bremner, who led the research project at Emory University Hospital in Atlanta.

So, the evidence is overwhelming that Accutane may cause depression and may lead to suicide.

Again, DO NOT use Accutane under any circumstances; and DO NOT allow your loved ones to use Accutane under any circumstances.

Period.

> *"There's no evidence linking the drug to so much as a single suicide . . . unless you count non-causal associations, rumor, innuendo, and the efforts of lawyers and politicians."*

Accutane Does Not Cause Suicide

Michael Fumento

In the following viewpoint, Michael Fumento argues that the anti-acne medication Accutane is the victim of bad publicity. He says the medication has been used beneficially to treat millions of people, mostly teens, who suffer from a severe form of acne. Fumento lays out the reasons why he believes it is incorrect and unfair to say that Accutane causes suicide. Michael Fumento is a journalist specializing in science and health issues and is also the author of a number of books.

As you read, consider the following questions:

1. According to Fumento, what is the variety of acne that Accutane is used to treat?
2. What is AERS, and what is it used for?

Michael Fumento, "Bumps in the Night: The Accutane Story Is All Scare, and No Science," *Reason Online.* January 23, 2002. Copyright 2002 Reason Online. Reproduced by permission. Available at www.fumento.com/accutane.html.

3. What is the active ingredient in Accutane, and what vitamin is it derived from?

In the movie *One-Eyed Jacks*, Marlon Brando asks Marshall Karl Malden if he'll get a fair trial. "Oh sure, kid, sure," answers Malden, soothingly. "You're gonna get a fair trial. And then I'm gonna hang you! Personally!"

That pretty much sums up how everybody—but the patients themselves—have treated Roche Laboratories' acne drug, Accutane.

Recently the capsules were back in the news after a 15-year-old St. Petersburg, Florida boy named Charles Bishop stole a light plane and flew it into the 28th floor of a 42-story Tampa building. A sample of the media coverage:

- *CNN Live Today*: "Tampa Authorities Say They Found Acne Drug Accutane at Home of Teen Pilot Charles Bishop"

- ABC's *Good Morning America*: "Charles Bishop May Have Used Accutane before Crash"

- *United Press International*: "Teen Pilot Had Accutane Prescription"

- *Newsday*: "Pilot's Acne Drug Linked to Suicides"

- And this one says it all, from London's *The Mirror*: "Plane Boy Drugs Link"

More bizarre yet: Police found a note on Bishop's body expressing sympathy for Osama bin Laden and support for the September 11 attacks.

Clearly something was troubling this young man, but it wasn't Accutane. As only a handful of media outlets bothered to report a week later, an autopsy showed no trace of the drug in the boy's system.

Undeserving Reputation

Nonetheless, the story will add to the undeservedly bad reputation of a drug used by 5 million Americans and 7 million others worldwide since 1982 to combat one of the most disfiguring forms of acne, the "severe recalcitrant nodular" variety. Yet there's no evidence linking the drug to so much as a single suicide (much less support for international terrorism)—unless you count non-causal associations, rumor, innuendo, and the efforts of lawyers and politicians.

Three things quickly sent Accutane down the road to infamy, despite clear evidence of its tremendous benefits to users. The first is that it was known from the beginning that Accutane is a powerful teratogen, meaning it causes birth defects. It's been labeled as such since its introduction, and Roche has worked aggressively (albeit not completely successfully) to prevent any woman who might possibly be pregnant or become so soon from getting a prescription. Medically, teratogenicity has nothing to do with depression or thoughts of suicide. But this gave the drug immediate notoriety.

From its launch, doctors were keeping a sharp eye out for any other possible serious side effect and reporting those possible connections to the [U.S. Food and Drug Administration] FDA under its adverse event reporting system (AERS).

Bad Publicity

"When there's public awareness or publicity about a drug for any reason, there may be an increase in reports because people may not have otherwise thought about associations," points out FDA spokeswoman Kathleen Kolar. Nevertheless, she immediately adds that while "Accutane is safe and effective when used as directed, any drug that has had that many warnings does merit concern."

Hmm . . . In any case, this concern led the FDA to require that Roche warn on the drug's label that it may cause "depression, psychosis, suicidal ideation, suicide, and attempts at suicide." This in turn no doubt has and will lead to more adverse event reports.

Indeed, according to Roche spokeswoman Gail Safian, the Tampa incident is being reported to the FDA as an Accutane-related suicide, notwithstanding that there's no evidence Bishop ever took the drug. All the stories that fingered Accutane in his death will probably lead to more adverse reports.

Teens with Acne Prone to Depression

The second association between Accutane and suicide is that the drug is used primarily by people whose age group is especially prone to suicide. According to the U.S. Centers for Disease Control and Prevention in Atlanta, for persons "15–24 years old, suicide is the third leading cause of death, behind unintentional injury and homicide."

And the problem is getting worse. "From 1952–1995, the incidence of suicide among adolescents and young adults nearly tripled," says the CDC. "From 1980–1997, the rate of suicide among persons aged 15–19 years increased by 11% and among persons aged 10–14 years by 109%." Accutane, introduced in 1982, arrived about 30 years too late to have been the cause of this increase.

The third association between Accutane and suicide is that researchers have found what appears to be a cause-and-effect link between even mild acne and depression. You might expect that Clearasil users have a higher rate of suicide. Nevertheless, while the overall rate of suicide in the general population is about 11.1 per 100,000; that of Accutane users, according to a Roche survey, is 1.8 per 100,000. There have been about 90,000 U.S. suicides since 1982 compared to 167 FDA adverse reports for Accutane-related suicides.

Moreover, nobody has found any kind of biological plausibility for how Accutane might even cause depression. The active ingredient in Accutane (isotretinoin) is a Vitamin A de-

Accutane Works and Is Safer than You Think

Isotretinoin, sold under the brand name Accutane, is the only drug that can cure acne, but it can cause horrible birth defects when taken by pregnant women. Reports from Britain and Israel show that Accutane otherwise is much safer than we used to think. . . .

In the British study, 93 percent of the people taking Accutane reported no long-term side effects. The British researchers reported that 2 percent suffered muscle aches at follow up, and 5 percent suffered from dry mouth. Fewer than 1 percent claimed that they had dry eyes and skin and joint pains. Higher doses were not associated with more side effects. The authors concluded that their study showed that isotretinoin is a safe drug with no serious long-term side-effects. However, it causes birth defects when taken during pregnancy.

A study from Israel also shows that Accutane is far safer than many doctors think.

Gabe Mirkin, "Is Accutane Safe?" Ezine Articles,
December 11, 2005. Available at http://EzineArticles.com.

rivative and overdoses of Vitamin A can be toxic. But there is no evidence that hypervitaminosis A can cause psychiatric reactions.

Lawyers and Politicians Contribute to Hysteria

Another important contributor to the hysteria are the sharks in suits. After all, suicide cases are natural heart-tuggers and you never know when you'll get lucky before a judge or jury. If you go to a Web site with an innocuous-sounding name like http://www.accutane_suicide_help.com/ you'll find you've actually come across a lawyer-referral service.

It's indicative of the weak case against Accutane that one of the most powerful indictments came from the allegations of a single man with no medical background and a powerful motive to lay blame. In late 2000, the son of Rep. Bart Stupak committed suicide. As do so many grieving parents whose children have taken their own lives, Stupak sought desperately for a reason. What he found was that Bart Jr. had been taking Accutane.

Stupak's accusation, though, didn't just go to the FDA; it was broadcast in his own press conference, in which the lawyer and former state trooper took on the role of both forensic specialist and epidemiologist. This in turn led to House hearings, plenty more media coverage, and no doubt more adverse event reports.

Vicious Cycle Accutane Will Never Escape

So it has been and always will be for Accutane. Bad publicity leads to more bad publicity which leads to even more bad publicity. It is a vicious cycle from which Accutane and Roche will never escape. There's a valuable lesson in here; but don't expect that anyone will learn it.

> *"The evidence shows that the presence of American troops is clearly the pivotal factor driving suicide terrorism."*

Foreign Occupation Is the Primary Cause of Suicide Terrorism

Scott McConnell Interview with Robert Pape

In the following viewpoint, Scott McConnell interviews Robert Pape, the author of an acclaimed book about suicide terrorism. Pape contends that the widely held belief that Islamic fundamentalism is the primary cause of suicide terrorism is wrong. Pape claims to have collected and analyzed the data of every completed suicide terrorist incident in the world since 1980. He concludes that foreign occupation is the key reason behind suicide terrorist incidents, and he suggests that the moment U.S. troops vacate the Arabian Peninsula, anti-American suicide terrorism will stop. Scott McConnell is a widely read columnist and one of the founders of American Conservative *magazine.*

As you read, consider the following questions:

1. What group does Pape say is the world leader in suicide terrorism? What country is the group from?

2. According to Pape, Osama bin Laden's speeches ad sermons call tremendous attention to what?

3. What is the "offshore balancing" strategy?

S cott McConell: *Your new book,* Dying to Win, *has a subtitle:* The Logic of Suicide Terrorism. *Can you just tell us generally on what the book is based, what kind of research went into it, and what your findings were?*

Robert Pape: Over the past two years, I have collected the first complete database of every suicide-terrorist attack around the world from 1980 to early 2004. This research is conducted not only in English but also in native-language source—Arabic, Hebrew, Russian, and Tamil, and others—so that we can gather information not only from newspapers but also from products from the terrorist community. The terrorists are often quite proud of what they do in their local communities, and they produce albums and all kinds of other information that can be very helpful to understand suicide-terrorist attacks.

Foreign Occupation, Not Fundamentalism Drives Suicide Terrorists

This wealth of information creates a new picture about what is motivating suicide terrorism. Islamic fundamentalism is not as closely associated with suicide terrorism as many people think. The world leader in suicide terrorism is a group that you may not be familiar with: the Tamil Tigers in Sri Lanka.

This is a Marxist group, a completely secular group that draws from the Hindu families of the Tamil regions of the country. They invented the famous suicide vest for their suicide assassination of Rajiv Gandhi in May 1991. The Palestinians got the idea of the suicide vest from the Tamil Tigers.

So if Islamic fundamentalism is not necessarily a key variable behind these groups, what is?

The central fact is that overwhelmingly suicide-terrorist attacks are not driven by religion as much as they are by a clear strategic objective: to compel modern democracies to withdraw military forces from the territory that the terrorists view as their homeland. From Lebanon to Sri Lanka to Chechnya to Kashmir to the West Bank, every major suicide-terrorist campaign—over 95 percent of all the incidents—has had as its central objective to compel a democratic state to withdraw.

That would seem to run contrary to a view that one heard during the American election campaign, put forth by people who favor Bush's policy. That is, we need to fight the terrorists over there, so we don't have to fight them here.

Since suicide terrorism is mainly a response to foreign occupation and not Islamic fundamentalism, the use of heavy military force to transform Muslim societies over there, if you would, is only likely to increase the number of suicide terrorists coming at us.

Osama Bin Laden Answered by U.S. Troops

Since 1990, the United States has stationed tens of thousands of ground troops on the Arabian Peninsula, and that is the main mobilization appeal of Osama bin Laden and al-Qaeda. People who make the argument that it is a good thing to have them attacking us over there are missing that suicide terrorism is not a supply-limited phenomenon where there are just a few hundred around the world willing to do it because they are religious fanatics. It is a demand-driven phenomenon. That is, it is driven by the presence of foreign forces on the territory that the terrorists view as their homeland. The operation in Iraq has stimulated suicide terrorism and has given suicide terrorism a new lease on life.

If we were to back up a little bit before the invasion of Iraq to what happened before 9/11, what was the nature of the agit-prop that Osama bin Laden and al-Qaeda were putting out to attract people?

Osama bin Laden's speeches and sermons run 40 and 50 pages long. They begin by calling tremendous attention to the presence of tens of thousands of American combat forces on the Arabian Peninsula.

In 1996, he went on to say that there was a grand plan by the United States—that the Americans were going to use combat forces to conquer Iraq, break it into three pieces, give a piece of it to Israel so that Israel could enlarge its country, and then do the same thing to Saudi Arabia. As you can see, we are fulfilling his prediction, which is of tremendous help in his mobilization appeals.

The fact that we had troops stationed on the Arabian Peninsula was not a very live issue in American debate at all. How many Saudis and other people in the Gulf were conscious of it?

We would like to think that if we could keep a low profile with our troops that it would be okay to station them in foreign countries. The truth is, we did keep a fairly low profile. We did try to keep them away from Saudi society in general, but the key issue with American troops is their actual combat power. Tens of thousands of American combat troops, married with air power, is a tremendously powerful tool.

Now, of course, today we have 150,000 troops on the Arabian Peninsula, and we are more in control of the Arabian Peninsula than ever before.

If you were to break down causal factors, how much weight would you put on a cultural rejection of the West and how much weight on me presence of American troops on Muslim territory?

The evidence shows that the presence of American troops is clearly the pivotal factor driving suicide terrorism.

Most Suicide Terrorists Are from Countries Hosting U.S. Troops

If Islamic fundamentalism were the pivotal factor, then we should see some of the largest Islamic fundamentalist countries in the world, like Iran, which has 70 million people— three times the population of Iraq and three times the population of Saudi Arabia—with some of the most active groups in suicide terrorism against the United States. However, there has never been an al-Qaeda suicide terrorist from Iran, and we have no evidence that there are any suicide terrorists in Iraq from Iran.

Sudan is a country of 21 million people. Its government is extremely Islamic fundamentalist. The ideology of Sudan was so congenial to Osama bin Laden that he spent three years in Sudan in the 1990s. Yet there has never been an al-Qaeda suicide terrorist from Sudan.

I have the first complete set of data on every al-Qaeda suicide terrorist from 1995 to early 2004, and they are not from some of the largest Islamic fundamentalist countries in the world. Two thirds are from the countries where the United States has stationed heavy combat troops since 1990.

Troops Lead to More Suicide Terrorist Incidents

Another point in this regard is Iraq itself. Before our invasion, Iraq never had a suicide-terrorist attack in its history. Never. Since our invasion, suicide terrorism has been escalating rapidly with 20 attacks in 2003, 48 in 2004, and over 50 in just the first five months of 2005. Every year that the United States has stationed 150,000 combat troops in Iraq, suicide terrorism has doubled.

So your assessment is that there are more suicide terrorists or potential suicide terrorists today than there were in March 2003?

I have collected demographic data from around the world on the 462 suicide terrorists since 1980 who completed the mission, actually killed themselves. This information tells us that most are walk-in volunteers. Very few are criminals. Few are actually longtime members of a terrorist group. For most suicide terrorists, their first experience with violence is their very own suicide-terrorist attack.

There is no evidence there were any suicide-terrorist organizations lying in wait in Iraq before our invasion. What is happening is that the suicide terrorists have been produced by the invasion.

Do we know who is committing suicide terrorism in Iraq? Are they primarily Iraqis or walk-ins from other countries in the region?

Our best information at the moment is that the Iraqi suicide terrorists are coming from two groups—Iraqi Sunnis and Saudis—the two populations most vulnerable to transformation by the presence of large American combat troops on the Arabian Peninsula. This is perfectly consistent with the strategic logic of suicide terrorism. . . .

De-Occupying the Arabian Peninsula Would Help

What would constitute a victory in the War on Terror or at least an improvement in the American situation?

For us, victory means not sacrificing any of our vital interests while also not having Americans vulnerable to suicide-terrorist attacks. In the case of the Persian Gulf, that means we should pursue a strategy that secures our interest in oil but does not encourage the rise of a new generation of suicide terrorists.

In the 1970s and the 1980s, the United States secured its interest in oil without stationing a single combat soldier on the Arabian Peninsula. Instead, we formed an alliance with Iraq and Saudi Arabia, which we can now do again. We relied on numerous aircraft carriers off the coast of the Arabian Peninsula, and naval air power now is more effective not less. We also built numerous military bases so that we could move large numbers of ground forces to the region quickly if a crisis emerged.

That strategy, called "offshore balancing," worked splendidly against Saddam Hussein in 1990 and is again our best strategy to secure our interest in oil while preventing the rise of more suicide terrorists. . . .

History of Suicide Attacks

The use of suicide attacks is not new. Japanese kamikaze pilots in World War II tried to cause maximum damage by crashing their fighter planes into U.S. ships. Walter Laqueur, an expert in the history of terrorism, also says that, for centuries, any attack on military or political leaders was a form of suicide because the act usually occurred at close quarters and brought swift and certain death for the killer.

One watershed came in 1983, when a Hezbollah operative drove his truck into the U.S. Marine barracks in Beirut, killing 241 U.S. service members in an attack that remains the deadliest terrorist strike on Americans overseas. Hezbollah would later carry out several dozen more suicide attacks.

Most experts agree that the modern style of suicide bombings first gained its greatest prominence outside the Middle East, in the island nation of Sri Lanka.

The Liberation Tigers of Tamil Eelam, popularly known as the Tamil Tigers, is an avowedly secular rebel movement of the country's Tamil ethnic minority. It carried out scores of suicide bombings from the late 1980s until a cease-fire in 2002. The conflict between the Tigers and the government, which is dominated by members of the Sinhalese majority, began in 1983 and claimed an estimated 65,000 lives.

Dan Eggen and Scott Wilson,
"Suicide Bombs Potent Tools of Terrorists,"
Washington Post, *July 17, 2005.*

Importance of Religious Differences

I not only study the patterns of where suicide terrorism has occurred but also where it hasn't occurred. Not every foreign occupation has produced suicide terrorism. Why do some and not others? Here is where religion matters, but not quite in the way most people think. In virtually every instance where an occupation has produced a suicide-terrorist campaign, there has been a religious difference between the occupier and the occupied community. That is true not only in places such as Lebanon and in Iraq today but also in Sri Lanka, where it is the Sinhala Buddhists who are having a dispute with the Hindu Tamils.

When there is a religious difference between the occupier and the occupied, that enables terrorist leaders to demonize the occupier in especially vicious ways. Now, that still requires the occupier to be there. Absent the presence of foreign troops, Osama bin Laden could make his arguments but there wouldn't be much reality behind them. The reason that it is so difficult for us to dispute those arguments is because we really do have tens of thousands of combat soldiers sitting on the Arabian Peninsula.

Preventing the Creation of Suicide Terrorists

Has the next generation of anti-American suicide terrorists already been created? Is it too late to wind this down, even assuming your analysis is correct and we could de-occupy Iraq?

Many people worry that once a large number of suicide terrorists have acted that it is impossible to wind it down. The history of the last 20 years, however, shows the opposite. Once the occupying forces withdraw from the homeland territory of the terrorists, they often stop—and often on a dime.

In Lebanon, for instance, there were 41 suicide-terrorist attacks from 1982 to 1986, and after the U.S. withdrew its forces, France withdrew its forces, and then Israel withdrew to just that six-mile buffer zone of Lebanon, they virtually ceased. They didn't completely stop, but there was no campaign of suicide terrorism. Once Israel withdrew from the vast bulk of Lebanese territory, the suicide terrorists did not follow Israel to Tel Aviv.

This is also the pattern of the second Intifada with the Palestinians. As Israel is at least promising to withdraw from Palestinian-controlled territory (in addition to some other factors), there has been a decline of that ferocious suicide-terrorist campaign. This is just more evidence that withdrawal of military forces really does diminish the ability of the terrorist leaders to recruit more suicide terrorists.

That doesn't mean that the existing suicide terrorists will not want to keep going. I am not saying that Osama bin Laden would turn over a new leaf and suddenly vote for George Bush. There will be a tiny number of people who are still committed to the cause, but the real issue is not whether Osama bin Laden exists. It is whether anybody listens to him. That is what needs to come to an end for Americans to be safe from suicide terrorism.

> "The time has come to address the real root cause of suicide bombing: elitist incitement by certain religious and political leaders who are creating a culture of death and exploiting the ambiguous teachings of an important religion."

Foreign Occupation Is Not the Primary Cause of Suicide Terrorism

Alan Dershowitz

In the following viewpoint, Alan Dershowitz contends that Islamic religious fundamentalism fuels suicide terrorism, not oppression or occupation by foreign armies. Dershowitz says that suicide bombers are typically educated, privileged, and wealthy young men and women taught to glorify the culture of suicide and incited to hate by Muslim religious leaders. Dershowitz says there is no evidence to support the claim that occupation and oppression cause suicide bombings. Alan Dershowitz is a Harvard professor, author, and lawyer.

Alan Dershowitz, "Does Oppression Cause Suicide Bombing?" *Jerusalem Post*, May 20, 2004. Reproduced by permission of the author. Available at http://www.alandershowitz.com/publications/docs/oppression.html.

As you read, consider the following questions:

1. What does "shahid" mean?

2. According to Dershowitz, what does Sheikh Muhammad Sayed Tantawi say about suicide bombings?

3. Suicide bombings in what country give Dershowitz reason to think that responsible Islamic leaders might come to understand that the real victims of the culture of death are their own people?

As suicide bombings increase in Iraq, in Saudi Arabia, and in Israel, more and more people have come to believe that this tactic is a result of desperation. They see a direct link between oppression, occupation, poverty, and humiliation on the one hand, and a willingness to blow oneself up for the cause on the other hand. It follows from this premise that the obvious remedy for suicide bombing is to address its root cause—namely, our oppression of the terrorists.

Suicide Terrorists Are Not Victims of Oppression

But the underlying premise is demonstrably false: There is no such link as a matter of fact or history. Suicide bombing is a tactic that is selected by privileged, educated, and wealthy elitists because it has proven successful.

Moreover, even some of the suicide bombers themselves defy the stereotype of the impoverished victims of occupation driven to desperate measures by American or Israeli oppression. Remember the 9/11 bombers, several of whom were university students and none of whom were oppressed by the US. They were dispatched by a Saudi millionaire named Osama bin Laden.

Bin Laden has now become the hero of many other upper-class Saudis who are volunteering to become shahids (martyrs) in Iraq, Israel, and other parts of the globe.

Majid al-Enezi, a Saudi student training to become a computer technician, recently changed career plans and decided to become a martyr; he crossed over into Iraq, where he died. His brother Abdullah celebrated that decision. "People are calling all the time to congratulate us, crying from happiness and envy. There are many young men who wish they could cross over into Iraq, but they can't. Thank G-d he was able to."

These rich kids glorify the culture of suicide, even in distant places. As Tufful al-Oqbi, a student at the elite King Saud University, described this situation, young people are wearing T-shirts with bin Laden's picture on them just the way people used to wear pictures of Che Guevara, the Cuban revolutionary. According to a recent news account, wealthy women students sport Osama bin Laden T-shirts under their enveloping abayas to show their approval for his calls to resist the United States.

Why do these overprivileged and well-educated young men and women support this culture of death, while impoverished and oppressed Tibetans continue to celebrate life despite their occupation by China for half a century?

Why have other oppressed people throughout history not resorted to suicide bombings and terrorism? The answer lies in differences among the elite leadership of various groups and causes. The leaders of Islamic radical causes, especially the Wahhabis, advocate and incite suicide terrorism, while the leaders of other causes advocate different means.

Leaders Incite Suicide Terrorism

Recall Mahatma Gandhi and Martin Luther King, Jr., whose people were truly oppressed but who advocated non-violent means of resistance. It is the leaders who send suicide bombers to blow themselves up. No suicide bomber ever sent himself to be blown up.

The bombers accept death because they have been incited into a frenzy of hatred by imams preaching "Kill the infidels." Sheikh Muhammad Sayed Tantawi, the leading Islamic scholar at the elite Al-Azhar University in Cairo (which is not occupied), has declared that martyrdom operations—which means suicide bombings—are the highest form of jihad and an Islamic commandment.

Even more mainstream role models, such as Yasser Arafat's wife, who lives in a multimillion-dollar residence in Paris, has said that if she had a son, she would want him to become a suicide bomber because there is no greater honor than to become a martyr.

Young children, some as young as 12 and 13, are incited and seduced into strapping bombs around themselves by these older and better-educated elitist leaders. The children are promised virgins in heaven, praise and money for their families here on Earth, and posters portraying them as rock stars. It is an irresistible combination for some, and the blame lies squarely at the feet of the elitists who exploit them, use them, and eventually kill them.

No Link to Occupation

There is absolutely no evidence to support the claim of a direct relationship between occupation and suicide bombing. If anything, occupation makes it more difficult to launch successful terrorist attacks. This is not to argue for occupation; it is to separate the arguments regarding occupation from the claim that it is the fact of occupation, and the oppression it brings, that causes suicide bombing.

Indeed, were Israel to end its occupation of Gaza and most of the West Bank (as I have long believed it should), it is likely that terrorism would actually increase as terrorist commanders secure more freedom to plan and implement terrorist actions. The same might well be true in Iraq, were the United States to pick up and run.

Rewards For the "Shahid"

The term "suicide attack" is misleading. In the eyes of the attacker and his community this phenomenon has nothing to do with committing suicide. . . . Indeed, committing suicide is forbidden in Islam. Instead, he is seen as a "shahid"—a martyr who fell in the process of fulfilling the religious commandment of "Jihad" (holy war).

Therefore, suicide attacks may provide the "shahid" and his family with many substantial rewards:

- The radical Islamic activists who decide to become "shahids" see themselves as martyrs who are fulfilling a divine command of protecting their religion from the attack by the infidels. . . .

- In some cases, the "shahid" is also seen as committing a patriotically altruistic act for his nation by carrying out a suicide attack. . . .

- In some cases, "shahids" come from a low social status background and by carrying out the suicide attack they improve their family's socioeconomic status after their death. . . .

- In addition to the religious mission and the family rewards, the "shahid" also receives some personal benefits (according to his belief). . . . [H]e earns eternal life in paradise, he is spared from suffering the horrific purification period in the grave . . . earns the loving kindness of 72 young virgins who will serve him in heaven. . . . [He] also earns the privilege of promising a life in heaven to 70 of his relatives and friends. . . .

Boaz Ganor, "The Rationality of the Islamic Radical Suicide Attack Phenomenon," International Institute for Counter-Terrorism. *March 21, 2007. Available at http://ict.org.il*

Islamic Fundamentalism Real Root Cause

The time has come to address the real root cause of suicide bombing: elitist incitement by certain religious and political leaders who are creating a culture of death and exploiting the ambiguous teachings of an important religion.

Abu Hamza—the cleric who tutored Richard Reid, the convicted shoe bomber—recently urged a large crowd to embrace death. Islamic young people are in love with death, claim some influential imams; but it is these leaders who are arranging the marriages between the children and the bomb belts.

Perhaps, now that suicide bombers have attacked Saudi Arabia, responsible Islamic leaders will better understand that it is their people who will be the ultimate victims of this tactically imposed culture of death.

Periodical Bibliography

The following articles have been selected to supplement the diverse views presented in this chapter.

Yvette Chau — "Do Accutane Side Effects Outweigh the Benefits of Taking the Drug?" *Ezinearticles.com*. January 27, 2006. Available at http://EzineArticles.com/?expert=Yvette_Chau

Elizabeth Cohen — "Push to Achieve Tied to Suicide in Asian-American Women," *CNN*. May 16, 2007. Available at http://www.cnn.com/2007/HEALTH/05/16/asian.suicides/index.html

Roger Cohen — "Terror and Demons," *New York Times*. October 8, 2007.

Ann Dowsett Johnston — "Stalking a Silent Killer," *Maclean's*. November 14, 2005.

Kate Stone Lombardi — "Countering Bridge's Dark Allure," *New York Times*. August 26, 2007.

Shiv Malik — "The Suicide Bomber in His Own Words," *New Statesman*. July 3, 2006.

Keith Mannes — "My Death: Darin Announced His Suicide Plans Online, and Followed Through. How Can I Help Our Small Town Cope with His Very Public Pain?" *Leadership*, www.leadershipjournal.net, (Carol Stream, IL). Fall, 2007.

Daphne Merkin — "Darkness Invisible: Owen Wilson's Very Public Suicide Attempt Outs an Unspoken Stigma," *New York Times*. September 16, 2007.

Sandra O'Loughlin and Steve Miller — "Marketers Struggle with the 'Dark' Side" *Brandweek*. February 20, 2007.

OPPOSING
VIEWPOINTS®
SERIES

CHAPTER 3

How Can Suicide Be Prevented?

Chapter Preface

College is a time of immense change and stress for many young people. Away from home and separated from support groups often for the first time in their lives, many college kids feel lonely and depressed. The pressures of achieving and competing against young people from all over the country are far different than the pressures they faced in high school. On top of all this, as most people enter college, they are experiencing one of the most difficult times in the cycle of life: the transition from adolescence to adulthood. The trials and tribulations of college and a difficult time of life can cause pain and mental anguish so severe some college students try to kill themselves. As the custodians of these young people, the question of what colleges should do to prevent their suicides is a topic of great debate. In an effort to avoid liability and maintain a positive campus atmosphere, some colleges have begun barring people who are potential suicide victims from living on campus. This has led to claims of discrimination and calls that colleges should do more to help suicide victims instead of locking them out of their dorm rooms.

The debate about a college's role in preventing the suicide of a student was brought to the public's attention when Elizabeth Shin committed suicide by self-immolation at the Massachusetts Institute of Technology (MIT). Shin was a sophomore on April 10, 2000, when she locked the door to her dorm room and lit herself on fire. Other dorm residents heard her crying and moaning and heard smoke alarms going off but could not get into her room. They had been concerned that Shin was going to harm herself. The night before, Shin had told one of them to erase her computer files because she wanted to kill herself. Once, she took an overdose of Tylenol 3. Another time she was found cutting herself, and in another incident she sent an e-mail to a teacher telling her that she wanted to kill herself. In the months before she took her life, she was seen by several concerned mental health professionals at MIT. But none of them followed up with her or took the steps to commit her for mental health treatment. They did prescribe antidepressants; however, they always allowed Shin to go home on the advice that she talk to her parents and seek treatment voluntarily. But Shin never let on to her parents how she was feeling, and none of the mental health professionals or Shin's college dean informed her parents of her troubles. Shin was pulled from her room and rushed to a nearby hospital with third-degree burns over 65 percent of her body. She died at the hospital a few days later.

Shin's parents were distraught and angry with MIT. In 2002, they filed a wrongful-death lawsuit against the school and several administrators and employees. They accused the school of "breaching its promise to provide an appropriate medical diagnosis and treatment of Shin, as well as reasonable security, emergency services, and level of care." In their lawsuit, Shin's parents alleged that despite numerous warning signs, such as sending e-mails to faculty members saying that she was depressed and wanted to kill herself, she received minimal attention. MIT counseling services either discharged her with minimal treatment or assumed she would talk to her parents about her difficulties and they would provide treatment for her. Shin's parents say that their daughter's death was the tenth of twelve suicides committed by MIT students since 1990 and was foreseeable by the school's administrators and its mental health services employees.

As part of its defense, MIT implied that Shin's mental health problems started before she entered, including a possible suicide attempt when Shin did not become valedictorian of her graduating class. According to MIT's lawyer Jeffrey Swopes, "the death of Elizabeth Shin was a tragedy—for this bright young woman, her family and friends, and all those at MIT who tried to help her . . . but it was not the fault of MIT or anyone who works at MIT." In April 2006, nearly six years after Elizabeth died, the Shins and MIT settled the case before trial.

The Shin MIT case alarmed university administrators across the country. Worried that they might be held liable for failing to prevent the suicide of a student, some began taking a zero-tolerance approach and banning students with suicide attempts or even those admitting they had suicidal thoughts from campus. A nineteen-year-old sophomore enrolled at Hunter College in New York City was locked out of her dorm and expelled after attempting suicide. Ethan Helfand, a student at George Washington University (GWU), was still in the hospital recovering from an attempted suicide when he was told to go to a hotel because he was forbidden from entering his dorm. The approach "is intended to save lives," although "it does appear insensitive" says Tracy Schario, from GWU. She goes on to say that, "suicidal behavior not only impacts the student but the environment around him. And I think it would be disingenuous to say litigation does not play into these decisions."

Some people, however, do not think colleges have a legal duty to prevent student suicides, and treating anyone who might kill themselves in a disciplinary manner is counterproductive. Thomas Szasz, a psychiatry professor at SUNY Upstate Medical University says "suicide is an act, not a disease. Preventing suicide—like preventing drunkenness—is the responsibility of the college student, not the college administration." Szasz continues, "colleges cannot compel students to report to mental health professionals, much less to undergo 'counseling'; they can only suspend or expel them. The assumption behind such therapeutic coercion is that it is an effective method of preventing suicide. There is not a shred of evidence for this. In fact, evidence indicates that coercive psychiatric suicide prevention increases the incidence of suicide." GWU student Helfand thinks the college's tactics will prevent some students from seeking help. Helfand returned to the GWU campus after a leave of absence and proclaims that no matter how depressed he gets, he will never set foot in the university health center again. Says Helfand, "Something might happen again and the university will say I have to leave."

Some students locked out of their dorms are suing colleges under the Americans with Disabilities Act (ADA) and the Fair Housing statutes. The Hunter College student took her case to court and argued that she was suffering from a disability and that instead of locking her out, the college should have attempted to help her. In August 2007, she was awarded a $65,000 settlement.

Many people sympathize with the situation that colleges are in. Michael Bogdanoff, writing in the *Legal Intelligencer*, says "colleges are in a no win situation. The college could offer support, but what if it is not good enough for the courts? What if the suicide is completed nonetheless? When do we get the parents involved? Do we not have the right to draft a housing code that protects students against the threat of suicide? Isn't there a time when a leave of absence is appropriate? After a suicidal gesture or attempt, isn't it fair to require students to show that they are not in jeopardy of hurting themselves or others before they are allowed to return to the community?" Bogdanoff thinks there are ways colleges can better handle the situation, such as getting emergency contacts from students—someone who can be informed in a suicide emergency without violating privacy laws—and by getting a troubled student's parents and friends involved in helping them. Other universities are finding a middle ground. The University of Illinois' suicide prevention program, which was initiated well before the Shin case, requires that students attend four counseling sessions following a suicide threat or attempt. If they fail to attend all four sessions, they may be forced to leave school. According to school officials, it has reduced suicides there by more than half. Says Paul Joffe, director of the program, "based on common wisdom, it doesn't make sense that it should work, but it does, students threatening to end it all still care about staying in school."

Suicide prevention is an important and difficult subject. As the debate about what colleges should or should not do to prevent suicides proceeds, the lives of many potential suicide victims hang in the balance. The authors of the viewpoints in the following chapter provide their opinions on what works and what does not work, and what should and should not be done, when it comes to preventing suicide.

> "Antidepressant treatment resulted in
> lower rates of suicide attempts after
> people went on to treatment."

Antidepressants Prevent Suicide

Ed Edelson

A controversial 2004 recommendation on antidepressant labeling from the U.S. Food and Drug Administration warned of the potential for an increased suicide rate among young people after being prescribed certain medications. In the following viewpoint, Ed Edelson reports that newer trials that focused on suicide attempts among more than 70,000 people show that prescribing antidepressant medication for people who are depressed does have the potential for reducing the number of suicide attempts. Ed Edelson is a HealthDay reporter.

As you read, consider the following questions:

1. What did the 2004 FDA warning on certain antidepressant drugs outline?

2. What was the pattern of suicide attempts among people in the 2007 trial who were prescribed antidepressant medication from their primary care physician, psychiatrist, or psychologist?

Ed Edelson, "Suicide Attempts Fall After Depression Treatment Begins," *HealthDay*, July 2, 2007. http://www.healthday.com/Article.aep?AID=606073.

3. What is the "worst treatment option of all" for depression according to Dr. Greg Simon?

Suicide attempts dropped among people with depression soon after they started treatment, either with antidepressant drugs or psychotherapy, a study of more than 109,000 patients shows.

FDA Warns Against SSRIs

The study results come after a controversial 2004 recommendation on antidepressant labeling from the U.S. Food and Drug Administration (FDA). That move slapped a strong "black box" warning on the labeling of drugs called selective serotonin reuptake inhibitors (SSRIs), which include Celexa, Paxil, Prozac and Zoloft.

The warning outlined the potential for an increase in suicidal thoughts among teenagers and young adults prescribed the medications. The warning also urged closer clinical monitoring of these patients.

However, "the FDA warning was based on placebo-controlled trials," noted lead researcher Dr. Greg Simon, a psychiatrist and researcher at Group Health, a Seattle-based non-profit health care system. "They did not look at suicide attempts, because they were too rare. In the whole group of studies the FDA looked at, there were only two suicide attempts," Simon said.

Trial Shows Treatment Reduces Suicide Attempts

The current trial, published in the July issue of the *American Journal of Psychiatry*, does focus on suicide attempts. It finds that pharmaceutical and psychotherapy treatments aimed at fighting depression reduce those attempts.

Simon's study looked at suicide attempts among more than 70,000 people who got an antidepressant prescription from their primary care physicians, almost 7,300 people who got prescriptions from a psychiatrist and more than 54,000 who started psychotherapy for the treatment of depression.

"The pattern of [suicide] attempts over time was the same in all three groups: highest in the month before starting treatment, next highest in the month after starting treatment, and declining thereafter," the report said. "Results were unchanged after eliminating patients receiving overlapping treatment with medication and psychotherapy. Overall incidence of suicide attempts was higher in adolescents and young adults, but the time pattern was the same across all three treatments," the study authors found.

The overall incidence of suicide attempts in the first six months was highest in those taking antidepressant drugs prescribed by a psychiatrist (1,124 attempts per 100,000), lower among those starting psychotherapy (778 per 100,000) and lowest of all among those who were taking antidepressants prescribed by a general practitioner (301 per 100,000).

Any Treatment Is Beneficial to Those Suffering Depression

The bottom line: "Our study indicates there is nothing specific to antidepressant medications that would either make large populations of people with depression start trying to kill themselves or protect them from suicidal thoughts," Simon said.

"Instead, we think that on average, starting *any* kind of treatment medication, psychotherapy or both, helps most people of any age have fewer symptoms of depression, including thinking about suicide and attempting it," he said.

The new report "is one of a couple showing that prescribing antidepressant medication for people who are depressed has the potential for reducing the number of suicide attempts," said Dr. J. John Mann, chief of the department of neuroscience at the New York Psychiatric Institute, New York City.

Do Antidepressants Cause Suicide?

First, and most importantly, the answer is no. No single thing can cause a complex behavior such as suicide (or violence), and to say that a drug, or event, or illness made someone do something is simplistic and, well, wrong. . . .

Asking the question simply, "do antidepressants cause suicide?" misses the meat of the argument. Cause? In whom? When, and under what circumstances? The real question is whether someone who is depressed is more likely to commit suicide off of the medicines than on them.

So while we ponder that question, let me offer a sobering statistic. Only 30% of the people who committed suicide had seen a psychiatrist in the past year. That means 70% hadn't.

Chris Ballas, "Do Antidepressants Cause Suicide?"
HealthCentral.com, May 14, 2007.

Mann co-authored one such report, which relied on U.S. Veterans Administration data. "We found exactly the same thing" as the Simon report, Mann said. "Antidepressant treatment resulted in lower rates of suicide attempts after people went on to treatment."

Benefits Outweigh Risks

Such studies "suggest that these medications may be more beneficial than has been thought in the past," Mann said. "If there is a risk in these medications, it clearly is outweighed by the benefits. *No* treatment is the worst option of all."

Simon also pointed out that the FDA warning reduced use of SSRI drugs for treatment of depression, but it has not appeared to increase doctors' monitoring of young people who are taking the drugs. The standing recommendation for three follow-up visits to the therapist prescribing antidepressant drugs was observed in only 21 percent of cases, the researcher said.

"That is where we are poor in practice," Simon said. "My concern is that the practical impact of the warning was [only in] reduced rates of treatment."

> *"As a psychiatrist and medical expert, I have documented dozens of cases of individuals who have committed suicide or violent crimes while under the influence of the newer antidepressants."*

Antidepressants Cause Suicide

Peter Breggin

In the following viewpoint, Peter Breggin maintains that the class of antidepressants known as "selective serotonin reuptake inhibitors" (SSRIs) can cause violence and suicide. Breggin says that Prozac, Zoloft, and other SSRIs have the same effect on the brain as PCP, methamphetamine, and cocaine—illegal drugs known to cause violence and aggression. Breggin contends that the use of SSRIs should be avoided, and the public should be more informed about the potential life-threatening risks associated with them. Peter R. Breggin is a psychiatrist, author, and founder of the International Center for the Study of Psychiatry and Psychology (ICSPP) and the journal Ethical Human Psychology and Psychiatry.

As you read, consider the following questions:

1. According to Breggin, the FDA didn't say that antidepressants definitely cause suicide. What did they warn?

2. What was the percentage of depressed children on Prozac that developed manic reactions, according to one clinical study cited by Breggin?

3. What reason does Breggin provide to explain why people who are depressed often respond to placebos?

On March 22 the FDA issued an extraordinary "Public Health Advisory" that cautioned about the risks associated with the whole new generation of antidepressants including Prozac and its knock offs, Zoloft, Paxil, Luvox, Celexa, and Lexapro, as well as Wellbutrin, Effexor, Serzone, and Remeron. The warning followed a public hearing where dozens of family members and victims testified about suicide and violence committed by individuals taking these medications.

New Antidepressants Can Lead to Out-of-Control Behavior

While stopping short of concluding the antidepressants definitely cause suicide, the FDA warned that they might do so in a small percentage of children and adults. In the debate over drug-induced suicide, little attention has been given to the FDA's additional warning that certain behaviors are "known to be associated with these drugs," including "anxiety, agitation, panic attacks, insomnia, irritability, hostility, impulsivity, akathisia (severe restlessness), hypomania, and mania."

From agitation and hostility to impulsivity and mania, the FDA's litany of antidepressant-induced behaviors is identical to that of PCP, methamphetamine and cocaine—drugs known to cause aggression and violence. These older stimulants and most of the newer antidepressants cause similar effects as a result of their impact on a neurotransmitter in the brain called serotonin.

For more than a decade, I have documented in books and scientific reports how this stimulation or activation profile can lead to out-of-control behavior, including violence. Indeed, the FDA's conclusions seem drawn from my recent detailed review of studies pertaining to abnormal behavior produced by the newer antidepressants: "Suicidality, violence and mania caused by selective serotonin reuptake inhibitors (SSRIs): A review and analysis" published in the *International Journal of Risk and Safety in Medicine*. . . . I made a similar analysis in my most recent book on the subject, *The Antidepressant Fact Book*.

As a psychiatrist and as a medical expert, I have examined dozens of cases of individuals who have committed suicide or violent crimes while under the influence of the newer antidepressants such as Prozac, Zoloft, Paxil, Luvox and Celexa. In June in South Carolina, Christopher Pittman will go on trial for shooting his grandparents to death while they slept. Chris was twelve when his family doctor started him on Zoloft. Three weeks later the doctor doubled his dose and one week later Chris committed the violent acts. In other cases, a fourteen-year-old girl on Prozac fired a pistol pointblank at a friend but the gun failed to go off, and a teenage boy on Zoloft beat to death an elderly woman who complained to him about his loud music. A greater number of cases involve adults who lost control of themselves while taking antidepressants. In at least two cases judges have found individuals not guilty on the basis of involuntary intoxication with psychiatric drugs and other cases have resulted in reduced charges, lesser convictions, or shortened sentences.

Depression and Manic Reactions

The FDA includes mania in its list of known antidepressant effects. Manic individuals can become violent, especially when they are thwarted, and they can also "crash" into depression and suicidal states. They can carry out elaborate but grandiose and doomed plans. One clinical trial showed a rate of 6% manic reactions for depressed children on Prozac. None developed mania on a sugar pill. Even in short-term clinical trials,

She Became Edgy and Withdrawn

In July, Julie Woodward began attending a two-week group therapy program at nearby Horsham Clinic. A break-up with a boyfriend and conflicts with her parents had left her feeling withdrawn and in a struggle to maintain good grades. One condition of attending the program was taking antidepressants, Tom Woodward says. He and his wife didn't really like the idea, but were told they were "essential to treatment" and "very benign."

On day three of the program, Julie began taking 50 milligrams of Zoloft, and that night came the first signs of unusual behavior. Julie and her mother had a small dispute, and Julie roughly shoved her mother, an out-of-character act, Woodward says.

During the next few days, Julie became more edgy and withdrawn. On the evening of day six, she told her parents she wanted to stay home alone. But when they looked for her later that night, they couldn't find her. The next day, her father found her body hanging in the garage. One week after starting on Zoloft, she had taken her life.

Rob Waters, "A Suicide Effect?" San Francisco Chronicle. January 4, 2004. Available at http://sfgate.com.

1% or more of depressed adults develop mania compared to a small fraction on the sugar pill.

Although it is difficult to determine the rate at which the antidepressants cause relatively uncommon tragedies such as suicide and violence, we do know that they cause stimulant effects such as irritability and agitation in a large percentage of patients, often a third or more. Doctors who fail to recognize these reactions as drug-induced may mistakenly increase the dose of the antidepressant with disastrous results.

Doesn't Hurt to Look at Other Options

Little will be lost by minimizing the use of the newer antidepressants. While there is strong evidence that they cause suicide, there is no convincing evidence that they can prevent it. Many older antidepressants cause less stimulation and are equally or more effective in head-to-head clinical trials. Beyond that, a number of meta-analyses drawing data from multiple studies have shown that antidepressants are no better than a sugar pill. People who are depressed often respond to placebo because it gives them hope. Severe depression is essentially a feeling of profound hopelessness and despair that can best be addressed by a variety of psychotherapeutic, educational, and spiritual or religious interventions.

Unfortunately, there are also risks involved with stopping antidepressants. Many can cause withdrawal reactions that last days and sometimes longer, causing some patients to feel depressed, suicidal or even violent. Stopping antidepressants should be done carefully and with experienced clinical supervision.

As a first step in responding to this public health threat, we should follow the example of Great Britain whose drug safety agency recently banned the use of many of these drugs in children. Beyond that, the FDA and the medical profession must forthrightly educate potential patients and the public about the sometimes life-threatening risks associated with the use of antidepressant medications.

> "SSRIs [antidepressant] drugs are nei-
> ther the evil that many believe, nor the
> magical solution that many hoped."

Antidepressants Debate Underscores Need for Treatment

Robert Bazell

In the following viewpoint, Robert Bazell says neither side has it right in the antidepressant debate. Some doctors and scientists claim that the class of antidepressants known as selective seroto- nin reuptake inhibitors (SSRIs) can cause violence and suicide, while others believe these drugs successfully treat depression and prevent suicide. Bazell says Prozac and other SSRIs are not the menacing monsters many have made them out to be; the risk of suicide he says is tiny. On the other hand, SSRIs carry many other side effects and should not be dispensed so easily. The most important thing, says Bazell, is that depression should be better treated. Robert Bazell is the chief science and health correspon- dent for NBC News.

Robert Bazell, "Antidepressants Not As Good, or Evil, As Believed," *NBC News from www.MSNBC.com*, May 8, 2007. Copyright © 2007 MSNBC Interactive. Republished with permission of MSNBC.com, conveyed through Copyright Clearance Center, Inc. Available at www.msnbc.msn.com/id/18533399/.

As you read, consider the following questions:

1. What is the major advantage of SSRIs over earlier anti-depressants, according to Bazell?

2. According to Bazell, what does the psychiatrist Peter Kramer mean when he says "cosmetic psychopharmacology?"

3. According to Bazell, what percentage of children taking SSRIs have suicidal thoughts? What percentage of adults?

Antidepressant drugs have sparked some of the most contentious and long-running battles in the history of medicine. The Food and Drug Administration's (FDA's) decision last week to change the labels on the drugs is not likely to quiet the shouting.

Since October 2004 the FDA has required black-box warnings—the strongest alert of danger—on the medicines, noting a potential for young people taking antidepressants to have suicidal thoughts and behavior. With its latest move, the agency extended the warning to include 18- to 24-year-olds, but not to those age 25 and over. At the same time, the agency altered the label to note that "depression and certain other psychiatric disorders are themselves associated with increases in the risk of suicide."

So do antidepressants prevent suicide or cause it?

The FDA says they do both. That is only one of the many conflicts. One can also argue these drugs are used far too often in certain situations and far too little in others.

Prozac Becomes a Celebrity

The saga began in December 1987 when Prozac hit the market. It was the first in the class of drugs called SSRIs (Selective Serotonin Reuptake Inhibitors) that now includes Zoloft, Paxil, Effexor, Luvox and Lexapro. It's widely believed that SSRIs are designed from a firm understanding of the brain chemistry of depression, but, like most drugs, they were developed more through serendipity than science. Their mode of action resembles cocaine, ecstasy and methamphetamine, although they do not cause rapid euphoria or the difficult crash.

The major advantage of the SSRIs over earlier antidepressants is that it is almost impossible to overdose on them. They lack other severe side effects of earlier drugs such as toxic interactions with certain types of foods. There is no doubt SSRIs can effectively relieve depression for many people.

With the National Institute of Mental Health estimating that 14.8 million adult Americans suffer major depressive disorder, it is hardly surprising that Prozac and its chemical cousins became celebrities in the world of pharmaceuticals.

In 1989 Newsweek featured a Prozac capsule on its cover. In his 1993 best-seller "Listening to Prozac," psychiatrist Peter Kramer described patients who underwent transformations of their personalities and felt "better than well" on the drug. Kramer speculated about our culture "facing the prospect of cosmetic psychopharmacology," where people would be using medications for enhancement, not simply to treat depression or other mental illnesses.

In response to this groundswell of enthusiasm—as well as drug-company marketing—the uses for the SSRIs rapidly expanded far beyond depression.

"It's almost a misnomer at this point to call them antidepressants," says Dr. Joseph Glenmullen, a clinical instructor in psychiatry at Harvard Medical School. "They are used for anxiety, obsessive-compulsive disorders, gambling, even nail biting. They're sort of all-purpose 'feel better' medications."

Suicide Danger Real, But Tiny

While SSRIs are not as dangerous as their predecessors, they're still replete with side effects. Reports of people, especially youngsters, killing themselves while taking Prozac and other SSRIs were reported almost as soon as the medications ap-

Medicating Unhappiness?

Dr. Ronald Dworkin tells the story of a woman who didn't like the way her husband was handling the family finances. She wanted to start keeping the books herself but didn't want to insult her husband.

The doctor suggested she try an antidepressant to make herself feel better.

She got the antidepressant, and she did feel better, said Dr. Dworkin, a Maryland anesthesiologist and senior fellow at Washington's Hudson Institute, who told the story in his book *"Artificial Unhappiness: The Dark Side of the New Happy Class."* But in the meantime, Dworkin says, the woman's husband led the family into financial ruin.

"Doctors are now medicating unhappiness," said Dworkin. "Too many people take drugs when they really need to be making changes in their lives."

For Dworkin, the proof is in the statistics. According to a government study, antidepressants have become the most commonly prescribed drugs in the United States. They're prescribed more than drugs to treat high blood pressure, high cholesterol, asthma, or headaches.

In its study, the U.S. Centers for Disease Control and Prevention looked at 2.4 billion drugs prescribed in visits to doctors and hospitals in 2005. Of those, 118 million were for antidepressants. . . .

Adult use of antidepressants almost tripled between the periods 1988–1994 and 1999–2000.

Elizabeth Cohen,
"CDC: Antidepressants Most Prescribed Drugs in U.S.,"
CNN.com, July 9, 2007. Available at www.cnn.com.

peared. At first the drug companies and many psychiatrists wrote the suicides off as an inevitability in treating large numbers of depressed people, saying many of them would have killed themselves anyway.

But as media reports and lawsuits about the suicides proliferated, the FDA started to take the matter seriously and ordered a look at all the studies done on the drugs. It turned out to be a difficult task. Drug companies had carried out few studies in children. The studies in both adults and children usually lasted a short time—often only 12 weeks.

Ultimately, based on the available data, the FDA ordered black-box warnings on the medications for children in 2004 and for young adults in 2007. Most experts say the suicide danger is real and doctors need to monitor young patients closely, especially in the first few months of treatment. One hypothesis holds that as the drugs start to work, young minds become disinhibited just enough to start talking more about suicide and possibly attempting it.

As frightening as this side effect is, it is important to note it is tiny. Suicidal thoughts (and almost no actions) were recorded in 1.4 percent of children taking the drugs and 0.5 percent of the young adults.

Other Side Effects More Common

The biggest problem with the SSRIs is all the other side effects that are far more frequent: sleeplessness, anxiety, weight gain, nausea and very commonly, a loss of libido and difficulty achieving orgasm.

Dr. Peter Kramer told me recently that with the side effects as we now understand them, it would be wrong to use current antidepressants for the "cosmetic psychopharmacology" he speculated about in "Listening to Prozac."

"I just don't think doctors have the social permission now to treat things that fall shy of even minor mental illness," he said.

Not a Magic Bullet

To make matters worse, studies show that the drugs seldom work like magic bullets to alleviate symptoms in chronically depressed patients. Most need to try different drugs in varying doses until they get adequate relief.

"You can't just give these medicines and say 'come back in six months and tell me how you did.' These are serious drugs," Kramer said.

Unfortunately, in the real world of medical practice that is usually what happens. General practitioners with no special expertise write many of the prescriptions. Studies show that most patients simply stop taking the medications because they don't experience benefits and can't stand the side effects.

As a result, depression—a widespread illness that not only increases the risk for suicide, but also for heart disease, cancer and many physical ailments and social problems—remains vastly undertreated. Statistics show that when the FDA began debating the suicide risk for children in 2004, prescriptions for the drugs to adolescents fell, while the suicide rate, which had been declining for years, went up.

SSRIs drugs are neither the evil that many believe, nor the magical solution that many hoped. However many prescriptions may be written for frivolous uses, the overriding message from this debate should be that we need to do a far better job of treating depression, with and without the medicines.

> "How can we not routinely screen young people for mental illness when it is such an important cause of suffering and death?"

Screening Teenagers Can Help Prevent Teen Suicide

Richard A. Friedman

In the following viewpoint, Richard Friedman says that many teenagers suffer with depression and other mental illnesses and don't get the help they need. Tragically, some of these teens end up taking their own lives. Friedman thinks school-based screening programs like Teen Screen are an effective way to identify kids at risk for depression and prevent suicide. Friedman believes that screening programs do not infringe on parental rights—in fact he says the parents of most teen suicide attempters aren't even aware their teen is troubled. He also says any stigma associated with being positively identified as a suicide risk, is far less of a price to pay then death. Richard Friedman is a professor of clinical psychiatry and the director of the Psychopharmacology Clinic at Weill Medical College.

Richard A. Friedman, "Uncovering an Epidemic—Screening for Mental Illness in Teens," *New England Journal of Medicine*, vol. 355, December 28, 2006, pp. 2717–2719. Copyright © 2006 Massachusetts Medical Society. All rights reserved. Reproduced by permission.

As you read, consider the following questions:

1. According to Friedman, half of all serious adult psychiatric illnesses start by what age?
2. According to David Shaffer, Teen Screen is conducted in two stages. Describe the two stages.
3. According to Friedman, what is the chance that a teen has an anxiety, mood, or addictive disorder?

Courtney, a 15-year-old from Portland, Oregon, always knew she was different from the other kids. "I had a sense that something was going on, but I was afraid to say anything because I didn't know anyone else had a similar problem," she said. Like thousands of U.S. teens, Courtney participated in a mental health screening program that was offered in her school. "Teenagers have a hard time asking for help," she explained. "Without the screening, I'm not sure how I would have gotten the help I needed."

Before screening, Courtney was part of a silent epidemic of mental illness among teenagers. We know from the National Comorbidity Survey that half of all serious adult psychiatric illnesses—including major depression, anxiety disorders, and substance abuse—start by 14 years of age, and three fourths of them are present by 25 years of age. Yet the majority of mental illness in young people goes unrecognized and untreated, leaving them vulnerable to emotional, social, and academic impairments during a critical phase of their lives. Even those who receive treatment tend to do so only after a long delay: 6 to 8 years for patients with mood disorders and 9 to 23 years for those with anxiety disorders.

But it is not psychiatric morbidity that makes headlines; rather, it is the most extreme consequence of psychiatric illness: suicide. In the United States, suicide is the third-leading cause of death among persons 15 to 19 years of age. In 2005 alone, according to the Centers for Disease Control and Prevention, 16.9% of U.S. high school students seriously considered suicide, and 8.4% had attempted suicide at least once during the preceding year.

These grim statistics argue strongly for early detection and intervention and provide a rationale for mental health screening among teenagers. The premise is that the primary risk factors for suicide—mood disorder, a previous suicide attempt, and alcohol or substance abuse—can be identified and treated.

Courtney participated in TeenScreen, a large, school-based mental health screening program that was developed under the direction of David Shaffer at Columbia University. The screening is conducted in two stages: teens fill out a short questionnaire and are then interviewed by a master's level social worker or clinical psychologist, who verifies that a positive result is really clinically significant. If it is, the clinician recommends a more comprehensive psychiatric evaluation to the teen and his or her parents. The screening is voluntary and requires the active consent of the parents and assent of the teen. Screening results are confidential and are not shared with school officials or teachers. And since all teenagers who undergo screening also receive a follow-up interview, they cannot be identified by their peers as having screened positive, a system that preserves privacy.

In 2005, the program screened 55,000 young people in 42 states. "About one third of kids screened positive on the questionnaire, and one half of those—about 17%—were referred for further evaluation after the clinical interview," said Laurie Flynn, executive director of Columbia University TeenScreen.

There is substantial federal support and funding for such voluntary mental health screening programs. In 2003, the President's New Freedom Commission on Mental Health specifically recommended increased screening for suicidality and mental illness. The commission promoted only programs that were voluntary and conducted with explicit parental consent. In 2004, the Garrett Lee Smith Memorial Act—named for Oregon Senator Gordon Smith's son, who committed suicide

Median Age at the Onset of Mental Disorders.	
Type of Disorder	Median Age at Onset year
Any disorder	14
Anxiety disorder	11
Mood disorder	30
Impulse-control disorder	11
Substance-use disorder	20

TAKEN FROM: Richard A. Friedman, "Uncovering an Epidemic—Screening for Mental Illness in Teens," *New England Journal of Medicine*, December 28, 2006.

when he was 21 years old—earmarked $82 million for youth suicide prevention and early intervention programs.

Not everyone approves of screening teens for psychiatric illness, however. One vocal opponent, Representative Ron Paul who is also a physician, tried unsuccessfully to pass legislation in 2005 banning the use of federal funds for such screening. "I believe the real goal is to make screening mandatory," Paul said. "The motivation might be sincere, but a lot of these folks in government are arrogant and don't believe that parents know what's best for their own kids."

Voluntary screening programs don't interfere with parental rights, but they might well threaten the common—and tragically false—belief that parents are always in a position to know when their child is in trouble and needs help. The fact is that children and teens are notoriously secretive about their own psychopathology: parents are unaware of 90% of suicide attempts made by teenagers, and the vast majority of teens who attempt suicide give no warning to parents, siblings, or friends. As Courtney put it, "You can be the greatest parent in the world and your kid could still have a serious problem you don't know about."

One 23-year-old woman I interviewed had been screened when she was 15. "I remember being really depressed and suicidal after my cousin sexually molested me," she said. "I couldn't tell my parents about it, and I took an overdose of pills that no one knew about." She says that her meeting with the screening staff helped her to feel comfortable telling her parents what had happened to her and how she felt. "They were shocked and had no idea what I had been going through," she said.

Given the unfortunate stigma that is still attached to mental illness, many observers see screening as an invasion of privacy. Yet suicide has public health implications, for it is, in a sense, contagious: there is ample evidence of suicide clusters among teens, and the relative risk of suicide after exposure to another person's suicide has been estimated to be two to four times as high among teens between the ages of 15 and 19 years as in other age groups.

Some critics worry that asking teens about their mood or suicidal feelings will cause distress or induce suicidal feelings or behavior. In fact, there is evidence to the contrary. In one study, teens were randomly assigned to undergo mental health screening with or without questions that probed suicidal feelings and behavior. The participants who were asked these questions were neither more distressed nor more suicidal than those who were not. In fact, among high-risk students with a known history of depression or suicide attempts, those who had been asked about suicidal thoughts and feelings actually felt less depressed and suicidal after the survey than those who had not been asked such questions.

Some question the effectiveness of mental health screening, arguing that there is little evidence that this intervention prevents young people from committing suicide. Proof that any intervention reduces suicide rates is a high bar to pass, however, since the rarity of suicide would necessitate that a very large population be studied over a long period in order to demonstrate efficacy. Still, preliminary evidence suggests that screening has some positive effects. In one follow-up survey of parents of children who were identified through Teen-Screen as having clinically significant psychiatric symptoms, including suicidal tendencies, 72% reported that their child was doing very well or had significantly improved and was seeing a mental health professional.

Finally, there is concern about the high sensitivity but relatively low specificity of the screening instruments, a combination that leads to many false positive results. The potential consequences of falsely identifying a teen as needing a more thorough psychiatric evaluation seem far less dire, however, than those of failing to identify a suicidal teenager. Stigma is real, but unlike suicide, it doesn't kill.

It is accepted medical practice for teenagers to get frequent physical checkups, even though the odds of finding a serious physical disease in this population are very small. In contrast, the chance that a teen has a treatable psychiatric illness (such as anxiety, mood, or addictive disorder) is nearly 21%. How can we not routinely screen young people for mental illness when it is such an important cause of suffering and death.

I believe that voluntary mental health screening of teens should be universal. But we need to go beyond school-based screening if we are optimally to reach young people who are at risk for psychiatric illness and suicide. Pediatric clinicians are in an ideal position to detect mental illness in young people, and they should be better trained to probe for and recognize the signs and symptoms of major psychiatric disorders.

Courtney put it bluntly: "I'm not sure where I would be today if I didn't get screened. I'm not even sure if I would be here at all."

> *"Teen Screen, also known as the Colum-*
> *bia suicide screen, is an illegitimate in-*
> *trusion on privacy which purports to*
> *be a suicide prevention assessment tool,*
> *but lacks any semblance of scientific*
> *validity."*

Screening Teenagers Does Not Prevent Teen Suicide

Ellen Liversidge

In the following viewpoint, Ellen Liversidge, speaking on behalf of the organization Alliance for Human Research Protection (AHRP), argues against Teen Screen and any government-sponsored mental health screening of children. Liversidge, speaking before the commissioners of the Food and Drug Administration, says Teen Screen is scientifically unsound and is nothing more than a marketing scheme to get more American kids on mind-altering drugs and boost profits for the pharmaceutical industry. Liversidge, a board member of AHRP, lost a son who suffered a severe side effect (profound hyperglycemia) while taking the antipsychotic drug Zyprexa.

Ellen Liversidge, "Testimony before the U.S. Food and Drug Administration, on Behalf of the Alliance for Human Research Protection," *www.FDA.gov*, November 2, 2005. Reproduced by permission of the author and the Alliance for Human Protection. Available at www.fda.gov/cder/ddmac/dtc2005/051102Transcript.pdf.

As you read, consider the following questions:

1. According to Liversidge, between 55 and 60 percent of foster children in at least three states are on psychotropic drugs. What three states does she mention, and at what age does she say some children are started on the drugs?

2. According to Liversidge, what is Teen Screen's predictive level? What is Teen Screen's false positive rate?

3. How many American children each year are prescribed mind-altering drugs, according to Liversidge?

I speak today on behalf of [Alliance for Human Research Protection] AHRP, and also on behalf of all the parents I have met whose sons and daughters have been lost to psychotropic drugs. We are a band of brothers and sisters . . . having had the worst possible thing in all the world happen to us and to our innocent children.

Most of all, it is for the innocent children that are alive that I speak today, giving you AHRP's position on the very nefarious direct to consumer advertising scheme called Teen Screen, dreamt up by pharma and funded by the federal government. This plan will give unvalidated questionnaires to all the teens in every high school in the country, providing many of them with false, possibly false, psychiatric labels, and referring them to a doctor for probable medication, thus creating a new market share for the industry.

AHRP's position on this scheme is as follows. The Alliance for Human Research Protection opposes government policies requiring or promoting mental health screening of America's infants, toddlers and school children. Our opposition is informed by scientific, legal, ethical and common sense consideration.

It's All About Selling More Drugs

Number one, the primary catalyst for both Teen Screen and for the prescribing guidelines, known as TMAP, is market expansion. Dr. Peter Weiden, who is a member of TMAP—it stands for the Texas Medication Algorithm Project—expert consensus panel has charged that the guidelines are based on opinions, not data, and that bias due to funding sources undermines the credibility of the guidelines since most of the guidelines' authors have received support from the pharmaceutical industry.

The invalid screening process of Teen Screen ensures that mostly healthy normal children will be brought into government subsidized mental health dragnet. Once children acquire a psychiatric label, they may be branded for life. For example, between 55 and 60 percent of foster children in at least three states—Texas, Massachusetts and Florida—are on psychotropic drugs starting as young as age three.

Some children are on multiple drug cocktails, as many as 16 drugs. The drugs that are recommended by TMAP are both dangerous and often ineffective. They all carry black box warning labels.

Scientifically Invalid

Two, the diagnostic criteria upon which mental health screening instruments rest are scientifically invalid, vague and entirely open to subjective interpretation. Teen Screen was tested on 1,729 children in seven New York City schools using passive parental consent and teen active consent, which is legally invalid.

Teen Screen is fraught with suggestive insinuations of failure and self doubt. Such questions can lead vulnerable teenagers to obsess about perceived inadequacies that might lead them to develop low self esteem that could give rise to anxiety, withdrawal and emotional problems.

By raising the possibility that suicide may be an option, and that's one of the questions, screening might lead to suicidal thinking, as happens in Japan's Internet suicide clubs.

Teen Screen Pill-Pushing Squad

Enough cannot be said when it comes to the power of mental persuasion with kids. Most children feel lonely, depressed, like they don't fit in, like they are different than others, like they are not smart enough, good-looking enough, or popular enough at one time or another. This is normal thinking for all adolescents.

The Teen Screen pill-pushing squad takes advantage of normal and vulnerable kids when it goes into schools with a survey that asks them loaded questions about these normal notions and feelings, forever planting in their minds that such thoughts are abnormal.

Evelyn Pringle, "No Child Left Unmedicated:
Teen Screen, State-Drugging and Suicide,"
counterpunch.org, May 21–22, 2005. Available at
www.counterpunch.org.

Teen Screen questions are so vague, suggestive and broad that most normal teens are mislabeled as mentally ill.

Teen Screen, also known as Columbia suicide screen, is an illegitimate intrusion on privacy which purports to be a suicide prevention assessment tool, but lacks any semblance of scientific validity.

Indeed, the results of the study by Dr. David Schaeffer, chairman of child and adolescent psychiatry at Columbia University who is credited with developing and promoting Teen Screen showed that of 1,729 New York City high school students who were screened using the questionnaire, 475 students tested positive.

Number three, mental health screening is gambling with children's normal development. Teen Screen promoters fail to disclose that the risk for children who are screened to be falsely labeled as suicidal or mentally ill is 84 percent.

Falsely Marketed As a Suicide Prevention Tool

Number four, despite its proven unreliability as a predictive tool, and no evidence that mental health screening prevents suicide, Teen Screen promotes itself in direct to consumer marketing advertisements as a suicide prevention tool, proving that science is no deterrent to a marketing strategy.

The Teen Screen website states: We are running public service advertisements in the *New York Times* and the *Washington Post* to raise awareness of our new report, entitled, "Catch Them Before They Fall."

Catch Them Before They Fall is a marketing pitch much like pharmaceutical company advertisements that refer to unsubstantiated chemical imbalances. Teen Screen promoters are misinforming public health policymakers, school officials, families and teens by mischaracterizing their experimental, scientifically invalid questionnaire as a proven suicide prevention strategy, when their own research refutes such claims.

Teen Screen's low predictive level, shown to be only 16 percent, will result in falsely 84 percent of children who test positive as mentally ill or suicidal.

As acknowledged by Dr. Schaeffer, such a high rate of false positives could reduce the acceptability of a school-based prevention program.

Number five, coercive mental health screening and forced drugging is already happening to children in the United States. Current estimates are that each year 8 million American children, or about 10 percent of the school age population are prescribed mind-altering drugs. . . .

Teen Screen Trying to Circumvent Parental Consent

AHRP opposes psychiatric screening of children without active, informed parental consent. Consent of parents must be documented and given voluntarily without a hint of coercion. Teen Screen has attempted to sidestep parental consent by claiming passive parental consent, which is invalid.

Teen Screen is being sued in federal court by the parents of 15-year-old Chelsea Rhodes for violating their constitutional rights by failing to inform them that their child would be screened, and for failing to obtain parental consent. . . .

The FDA bears responsibility for failing to stop an unethical drug marketing strategy that is increasing the risk of serious harm for healthy children who are being misprescribed psychoactive drugs on the basis of an invalid screening tool that was being promoted with false claims.

According to its website, as of October 25th of this year [2005], Teen Screen is actively operating at locations 460 in 42 states and Washington, D.C.

> *"Until the cause of seeking help for those considering suicide reaches the proportions of prevention that heart disease and cancer already have, the gulf between suicide and prevention will be as wide as the bay the Golden Gate spans."*

More Needs to Be Done to Prevent Suicide

Dave Kitchell

In the following viewpoint, Dave Kitchell asserts that society must do more to understand and prevent suicide. Kitchell hopes that a documentary about those who end it all by jumping from the Golden Gate Bridge might lead to more discussions about suicide prevention. Suicide affects far too many young people, says Kitchell. Dave Kitchell is a staff writer for the Pharos-Tribune *in Logansport, Indiana.*

As you read, consider the following questions:

1. According to Kitchell, what are the two most troubling aspects of suicide?

2. What organization does Kitchell mention that has a Web site about teen health issues and suicide?

3. According to Kitchell, what past event can provide great lessons about suicide?

Alfred Hitchcock's chilling drama "Vertigo" featured actress Kim Novak driving to the pier beneath the Golden Gate Bridge and jumping into the bay before a private detective played by Jimmy Stewart pulled her to safety.

The tip-off for Stewart that her suicide attempt was phony in that classic is that Novak's character chose the pier beneath the bridge instead of the bridge deck. It was all part of an elaborate plot to cover up the murder of Stewart's old college chum.

For so many others, the bridge that represents one of the world's engineering marvels is their gateway to ending it all, and there is nothing phony about it. The plots are personal and the tragedies mount every year.

The Bridge

This week, a new documentary titled simply "The Bridge" is being released on DVD, and for those who have not seen portions of it or an interview with its producer, it's worth examining. "The Bridge" chronicles the attraction of the Golden Gate as a place for those who want to end their lives, seemingly as people drive or walk past the beams and railings.

If you've ever seen the sunset from Golden Gate Park or the Presidio, it's hard to imagine anyone would want to give up the chance to see another one like it, let alone years of them. But suicide is not about views from a place where Tony Bennett permanently keeps his heart. It's about depression and the treatment of it.

"The Bridge" may lead to more safeguards on the Golden Gate to make it more difficult for anyone to attempt suicide. The jury is still out on the possibility that "The Bridge" will lead to more deliberative discussions about what can be done to empower those who can have a hand in preventing deaths.

Suicide: Cost to the Nation

- Suicide takes the lives of more than 30,000 Americans every year.

- Every 18 minutes, another life is lost to suicide.

- Every day 80 Americans take their own lives, and over 1,900 Americans visit Emergency Departments for self-inflicted injury (National Hospital Ambulatory Medical Care Survey, total 706,000).

- Suicide is now the 11th leading cause of death in Americans.

- For every two victims of homicide in the U.S. there are three persons who take their own lives.

- There are now twice as many deaths due to suicide as to HIV/AIDS.

National Strategy for Suicide Prevention
"Suicide: Cost to the Nation," U.S. Department of Health and Human Services. *Available at http://mentalhealth.samhsa.gov.*

Perhaps that time has finally come, ironically at a time when Jack Kevorkian, the Michigan physician known for promoting assisted suicide for the terminally ill, has been released from prison. Oregon is the only state where assisted suicide is legal.

Suicide: Often Invisible and Often Affecting the Young

Probably the two most troubling aspects of suicide are that help is available for those with depression, but the lack of acknowledgment of the problem is part of the problem. In some criminal cases, suspects often take their own lives when they are trapped. But in most other suicides, the incident itself is never reported out of respect to the person or the person's family. It may be appropriate, but at the same time, it allows the problem to exist invisibly as a cause of death that is as lethal as any other.

The second troubling aspect is that so many young people are affected by suicide. It remains one of their top 10 causes of death. The Nemours Foundation, which has a Web site for teen health issues, has information about suicide and help for those who want it or need it.

For those who have ever known a high school where a young person committed suicide and friends followed suit, the shock is overwhelming. According to the foundation, drugs and alcohol can both play an active role in creating suicidal scenarios. At a point when most people have their entire lives ahead of them, too many give up, sensing only that there is heartbreak, hardship and disappointment in store. The great bard William Shakespeare may have gotten it wrong in "Romeo and Juliet" and may have rewritten his classic had he known so many young people would die at their own hand.

While the debate on assisted suicide for the terminally ill may evolve for years as life expectancy increases, there shouldn't be a debate about knowing the warning signs of depression.

Perhaps the great lesson about suicide came at the end of the roaring '20s when the stock market crashed on that fateful day in October of 1929. Windows opened and brokers, as legend has it, jumped to their deaths. The gilded, golden era of greatness had come to an end, or so it seemed. That's something to think about during these times when the stock market continues to set new records. Failure is temporary, but death is permanent.

Need More Prevention

And so, too, is the case with many problems confronting those who are contemplating an end. Until the cause of seeking help for those considering suicide reaches the proportions of prevention that heart disease and cancer already have, the gulf between suicide and prevention will be as wide as the bay the Golden Gate spans.

A new golden gate over that gulf is long overdue.

> *"We've got to do something very quickly and the most important thing we can do is reduce our numbers."*

Suicide Should Not Be Prevented

Chris Korda

In the following viewpoint, Chris Korda says that he supports suicide and euthanasia because humans are overpopulating and killing the earth. Korda believes that in the near future humans will deplete all of Earth's resources and exterminate many of Earth's species. There will be so much suffering, says Korda, that many of us will wish we had committed suicide. Korda supports suicide, euthanasia, abortion, and any other method that reduces the number of humans on the earth. Chris Korda is the son of author Michael Korda and the founder of the Church of Euthanasia.

As you read, consider the following questions:

1. How much does the population increase each year, according to Korda?

2. According to Korda, Church of Euthanasia members take a lifetime vow not to do what?

Chris Korda, "Editorial: Snuff It #4," *www.ChurchofEuthanasia.org*, reproduced by permission of the author. Available at www.churchofeuthanasia.org/snuffit4/editor.html.

3. According to Korda, in 2010, what will the Earth's population be?

Let me start by asking you a question. If you don't know, just guess, how long—months, weeks, days, hours, minutes, seconds—how long do you think it takes for the human population to increase by one million? Net increase.

Okay, I'll give it to you, it's four days. Four days, a quarter million per day, if you do the math, that comes out to *95 million people per year*, and just for a reference, 95 million is the population of Mexico, so next time you look at a map of the world, look at Mexico, and imagine the human population increasing by Mexico, every year.

Human Population Growth Is Killing the Planet

What do we do with all those people? They all need to eat, they all need houses, clothes, TVs, cars, and every other damn thing, who are *we* to say they shouldn't have them, and what's the result? The global environmental crisis. Massive species extinction. *Ecocide.* In the United States alone we lose an acre of trees every eight seconds. Worldwide, we're now losing an entire *species* every 40 minutes, that's up from every sixty minutes in the 1970's, and in the tropical rainforest we're losing a species every *fifteen minutes*. By some estimates we've already wiped out one third of the species on earth. Those species are *gone*, they're not coming back, this isn't some cute nature show on television, this is *real*. In terms of sheer power, this is our great accomplishment: severely damaging the chemical and organic structure of an entire planet, including the oceans and the atmosphere. We've got to do something, very quickly, and the most important thing we can do is *reduce our numbers*. It's something each one of us can do, it doesn't require special training, and that's why I, myself, and every one of the Church of Euthanasia's members have taken a *lifetime vow to not procreate*.

Why Support Suicide and Euthanasia?

Now people say to me, population reduction is one thing, but how can you support suicide and euthanasia, isn't that going too far, and I say this: right now, one third, that's a rough figure, it's probably higher, one third of the people on this earth are going to bed hungry every night. Does this surprise you? Maybe you're lucky: maybe you live in a country that still has some topsoil, or maybe your country steals food from everyone else. Don't get too smug, though, because simple arithmetic says the population will reach *8 billion* by 2010. Now that's well within my, and many of your lifetimes, and I'm telling you that if we, as *individuals*, allow that to happen, we are going to see suffering on a scale we can't even imagine yet, even right here, in the United States, and some of you are going to wish you had killed yourselves, because this planet is going to be a very grim and frightening place. It already is for most people.

Save the Planet, Kill Yourself

So that's why I say "save the planet, kill yourself." Because it really has come to this, and if you've had enough, and you want to get out of the game, and you honestly believe that's the best thing you can do for yourself and for the planet, I, Rev. Chris Korda, am not going to stand in your way. I'll make you a Euthanasian saint. And if no one listens to me, and the population keeps on growing, until there's no trees, and no hope, I'll join you. I think about it every day, and I feel *shame*. I'm ashamed of the way humans have behaved, especially *American* humans. When I look at the ugliness Americans have created in just two hundred years, and when I read about the "savages" we've exterminated to make room for our so-called civilization, *I feel suicidal rage*, and that's okay, because that's what the Church of Euthanasia is all about.

Now suppose, for the sake of argument, we divide people into two groups: those who think there are too many of us,

Not Enough Water

Water is a source of growing tension. Although much has been said about the conflicts between and among countries over water resources, some of the most bitter disagreements are taking place within countries where needs of local populations are outrunning the sustainable yield of wells. Local water riots are becoming increasingly common in countries like China and India. In the competition between cities and the countryside, cities invariably win, often depriving farmers of their irrigation water and thus their livelihood.

The projected addition to the earth's population of 3 billion people by 2050, the vast majority of whom will be added in countries where water tables already are falling and wells are going dry, is not a recipe for economic progress and political stability. Continuing population growth in countries already overpumping their aquifers and draining their rivers dry could lead to acute hydrological poverty, a situation in which people simply do not have enough water to meet their basic needs.

Reversing this situation depends on quickly slowing population growth. Otherwise the resulting political instability could soon eclipse terrorism as a threat to society.

Lester Brown, Adopted from Chapter 2:
Stopping at 7 Billion in Outgrowing the Earth
New York: W.W. Norton & Co., 2005.
Available at http://earth-policy.org.

and those who think there aren't enough. If you think there are too many of us, why not take some personal responsibility for it? Maybe we're the church for you. But if you think there's not enough of us, consider your allies. The people who oppose euthanasia, and say it's morally wrong, are very often the same people who oppose abortion; they're the same people who oppose contraception and family planning; they've opposed sex for pleasure for a thousand years, and you know who these people are, they are the *Catholic church and the fundamentalist christians.* Their religious teachings have been a disaster for the planet, and we cannot allow them to dominate us any longer. They're the *real* sinners, and they can't help themselves, so we have to help them: we have to *lead by example.*

Lead by Example

How do we lead by example? By practicing sex for pleasure, it's a revolutionary act, remember Joycelyn Elders [U.S. Surgeon General under President Bill Clinton] she wanted to teach masturbation and look what happened to her . . . By showing the maximum compassion for *all* beings, we can start by not eating their flesh, why are we feeding most of our grain to cattle when people are starving. . . By supporting abortion, we're *not* pro-choice, we're pro-*abortion*, why isn't it *free*, it's every woman's sacred right . . . By supporting Dr. Jack Kevorkian and the right to die, and above all by *choosing to not procreate,* until their churches are empty and ours is full, until the population is reduced to a sustainable level, and balance is restored between ourselves and every other species on this beautiful, living planet.

Periodical Bibliography

The following articles have been selected to supplement the diverse views presented in this chapter.

Alex Berenson and Benedict Carey — "Experts Question Study on Youth Suicide Rates," *New York Times*. September 14, 2007.

Deeanna Franklin — "Education Is Key to Suicide Prevention on Campus," *Internal Medicine News*. December 15, 2004.

Alex Kingsbury, Silla Brush, Elizabeth Weiss Green, and Bret Schulte — "Toward a Safer Campus," *U.S. News & World Report*. April 30, 2007.

Tracey Mitchell — "Tracey Mitchell interviews Kate Bornstein, author of Hello Cruel World: 101 Alternatives to Suicide for Teens, Freaks, and Other Outlaws," *Briarpatch*. September/October 2007.

Richard C. Morais — "It's Called Depression, Dude!" *Forbes*. September 3, 2000.

Julie Rawe and Kathleen Kingsbury — "When Colleges Go on Suicide Watch," *Time*. May 22, 2006.

Amanda Schaffer — "Stopping Suicide 101," *Slate*. May 26, 2006.

David Shern — "Are Warnings on Antidepressants Backfiring?" *Pediatric News*. October, 2007.

Deborah Sontag — "Who Was Responsible for Elizabeth Shin?" *New York Times*. April 28, 2002.

Carol Vinzant — "Suicide Mission; Teens Are Screened for Many Conditions, But Rarely for a Real Killer," *The Washington Post*. February 25, 2003.

Should Doctor-Assisted Suicide Be Allowed?

Chapter Preface

Jack Kevorkian was the face of the assisted suicide movement in the 1990s. He invented a killing machine called the mercitron which incapacitated or debilitated people could use to take their own lives: All they had to do was flip a switch. From 1990 to 1998, Kevorkian and the mercitron assisted at least 130 people with their deaths: The first was Janet Adkins, the last was Thomas Youk. The TV news show *60 Minutes* broadcast Youk's death across the country, and the videotape was subsequently used to put Kevorkian behind bars for second-degree murder. Assisted suicide is not legal in Michigan, where Kevorkian lived, nor is it legal in any other state, except Oregon. His release from prison in 2007 had many people reflecting on his impact on the assisted suicide movement. There are those who think the assisted suicide movement was better off without Kevorkian, while there are others who think he is a hero.

Kevorkian, born in Pontiac, Michigan, in 1928 was always interested in death. After going to the University of Michigan medical school, he specialized in pathology, which is the branch of medicine that is concerned with the causes of death and disease and where doctors perform autopsies. In the 1970s, he founded a radical movement that made a case for allowing condemned criminals to choose death by irreversible general anesthesia. This would allow the harvesting of their organs for donation or the use of their entire bodies for medical experimentation. Kevorkian received very little support for his idea. After that, Kevorkian became interested in helping people die. He coined the term "medicide" to indicate mercy killing performed by a doctor, nurse, paramedic, physician's assistant, or medical technician. Kevorkian started advertising in Detroit newspapers in 1987 as a physician consultant for "death counseling."

Kevorkian became known as "Dr. Death." In 1990, Janet Adkins flipped the switch on the mercitron killing machine, receiving a lethal dose of potassium chloride and became the first person Kevorkian helped to die. After assisting Adkins, Kevorkian assisted many more people to die throughout the 1990s. He didn't assist people to die in secret; he publicized his mercy killing and received national attention. He had murder charges brought against him in Michigan numerous times, and the court cases typically garnered a flood of media attention. In one trial, Kevorkian showed up in a powdered wig. During another trial, he staged a hunger strike. In 1998, the television show *60 Minutes* aired a videotape of Kevorkian injecting potassium chloride into Thomas Youk, who suffered from amyotrophic lateral sclerosis (Lou Gehrig's Disease). The tape was used as evidence in a murder trial against Kevorkian, and he was finally convicted of second-degree murder and delivery of a controlled substance on March 26, 1999. At his sentencing, the judge told Kevorkian, "you had the audacity to go on national television, show the world what you did and dare the legal system to stop you. Well, sir, consider yourself stopped." Kevorkian was released from prison upon the order of Michigan governor Jennifer Granholm in June 2007 after serving eight years of a ten- to twenty-five-year sentence. Kevorkian said he publicized his mercy killings in order to bring attention to the "right to die" movement. But many people think the attention he drew was negative. The "right to die" movement includes groups such as the Hemlock Society, Compassion and Choices, and the Final Exit Network that seek to change American laws so that each person has the right to choose the time and manner of his or her own death. Upon his release from prison, Derek Humphrey, founder of the Hemlock Society, said, "I thank Dr. Kevorkian for the huge public interest he aroused in the 1990s on this issue, and he will go down in history as a major catalyst for reform via the media's fascination." But Humphrey also said, "many in the health profession were and are skeptical about Kevorkian's style of assisted deaths back in the 1990s. Patients flying into Michigan one day, and being found dead the next, is not their idea of caring, cautious medical practice." Bioethicist Arthur Caplan said, "Kevorkian's problem was and is that he likes death way too much. The enthusiasm he brought to his cause was always deeply troubling. No doubts, no ambivalence, ever seemed to cross his mind as he dispatched his victims. The fact that he helped some to die within hours of meeting them, the fact that he would turn a disabled man's death into a national spectacle by giving a tape of his murder to *60 Minutes*—never mind that they used it!—and the fact he never seemed to try particularly hard to talk those who came to him out of their decision to die made him morally suspect then and hardly worth hearing from now." Many people believe that Kevorkian was not good for the right-to-die movement.

However, there are those who think Kevorkian was a hero. Writing in the *British Medical Journal* in 1996, John Roberts and Carl Kjellstrand said, "Jack Kevorkian is a hero. No one has demonstrated any discernible motive from him except that he believes his work is right. Greed for money is absent because he has charged no fees. Greed for fame, too, seems unlikely because he has shunned the media except to explain his position. And no one has accused him of sadism in ending the lives and, according to him, the suffering of his patients." Werner Gomez, writing in the Cerritos College newspaper in 2005 said, "Dr. Death is a saint, and frankly, he should be celebrated as one of this nation's heroes. The man assisted 130 people in their suicides, allowing them to die in a peaceful and dignified manner. Instead, for all his efforts in helping people end their misery and their lives in a pain-free manner, he was thrown in jail."

No matter how he is thought of, Kevorkian will be known for having brought assisted suicide to the nation's attention. So far, only Oregon has legalized assisted suicide, doing so in

1994. However, there have been attempts to legalize assisted suicide in California, Hawaii, and Washington, and the issue is still hotly debated. The authors of the viewpoints in the following chapter provide their opinions on whether doctors should or should not help people to die.

| *"Dying patients should be empowered*
| *to control their dying process."*

People Should Be Allowed To Choose Doctor-Assisted Suicide

Kathryn Tucker

In the following viewpoint, Kathryn Tucker maintains that dying people should have the choice to hasten their death. Tucker says the experience in Oregon, the only state allowing assisted suicide to date, shows that patients are not abused or coerced into dying. She says that most Americans support assisted suicide. Without a legal option, says Tucker, terminally ill patients who find the dying process unbearable are forced to hasten their own death in secret, using crude "back alley" methods; or if they ask friends or family to assist them, put their loved ones at risk of criminal prosecution for their complicity. Kathryn Tucker is a law professor and the director of legal affairs for Compassion & Choices, a national nonprofit public interest organization dedicated to improving end-of-life care and expanding and protecting the rights of the terminally ill.

Kathryn Tucker, "Testimony Before the United States Senate Judiciary Committee, The Consequences of Legalized Assisted Suicide and Euthanasia," *www.Compassionand Choices.org*, May 25, 2006. Reproduced by permission of the author. Available at www.compassionandchoices.org/documents/KT_Judic_Testimony.pdf.

As you read, consider the following questions:

1. The *Glucksberg* and *Quill* Supreme Court cases were brought by what two groups of people in what two states? What did they challenge?

2. According to Tucker, how does someone qualify as "terminally ill" under Oregon's DIGNITY ACT?

3. According to a 1998 *New England Journal of Medicine* survey cited by Tucker, what had almost 30 percent of doctors received?

As Legal Director for Compassion & Choices, I speak on behalf of our supporters, who strongly believe, as do a majority of Americans, that dying patients should be empowered to control their dying process. Even with excellent pain and symptom control a fraction of dying patients will confront a dying process so prolonged and marked by such extreme suffering and deterioration, that they determine that hastening impending death is the least worst alternative.

I have some specialized expertise that I hope will be of use to this committee. I represented the patients and physicians in the cases *Glucksberg v. Washington* and *Quill v. N.Y.*, decided by the US Supreme Court in 1997, and represented the patients in the case decided by that court just this term, *OR et al v. Ashcroft/Gonzales*.

The *Glucksberg* and *Quill* cases were brought by terminally ill patients and physicians in Washington and New York against those States, challenging state laws criminalizing assisted suicide, to the extent it applied to mentally competent terminally ill citizens who wanted to hasten death. The plaintiffs claimed that the right to make this choice was protected under the federal constitution's guarantees of liberty and equality. These claims, successful in both federal Courts of Appeals, the Second and Ninth Circuits, were rebuffed by the US Supreme Court in a pair of rulings issued in June of 1997 because the Court believed that the issue should be addressed, in the first instance, by the states. The Court's decision encouraged the "earnest and profound debate about the morality, legality and practicality of physician assisted suicide" to continue.

Oregon's Experience

More than eight years of experience in the state of Oregon has demonstrated that risks to patients are not realized when a carefully drafted law is in place. In light of the Oregon experience, even previously staunch opponents have recognized that continued opposition to such a law can only be based on personal moral or religious grounds. The State of Vermont recently concluded, after thorough review of the Oregon experience, that: "**it is [quite] apparent from credible sources in and out of Oregon that the Death with Dignity Act has not had an adverse impact on end-of-life care and in all probability has enhanced the other options.**"

Arthur Caplan, Director of the Center for Bioethics at the University of Pennsylvania School of Medicine, after reviewing the Oregon data stated: "I was worried about people being pressured to do this. But this data confirms, for the seventh year, that the policy in Oregon is working. There is no evidence of abuse or coercion or misuse of the policy."

The American Public Health Association, in an amicus brief filed in the Supreme Court of the United States recently, advised the Court:

> Researchers have consistently found that experience in Oregon *does not* bear out concerns that physician-assistance 'would be disproportionately chosen by or forced on terminally ill patients who were poor, uneducated, uninsured, or fearful of the financial consequences of their illness.' . . .

Oregon's DIGNITY ACT

The DIGNITY ACT establishes tightly controlled procedures under which competent, terminally ill adults who are under the care of an attending physician may obtain a prescription for medication to allow them to control the time, place, and manner of their own impending death. The attending physician must determine, among other things, that the patient is mentally competent, an Oregon resident, and confirm their diagnosis and prognosis. To qualify as "terminally ill" a person must have "an incurable and irreversible disease that has been medically confirmed and will, within reasonable medical judgment, produce death within six months."

The attending physician must also inform persons requesting such medication of their diagnosis and prognosis, the risks and probable results of taking the medication, and alternatives to taking their own lives, including, but not limited to, hospice care and pain relief. A consulting physician must confirm the attending physician's medical opinion.

Once a request from a qualifying patient has been properly documented and witnessed, and all waiting periods have expired, the attending physician may prescribe, but not administer, medication to enable the patient to end his or her life in a humane and dignified manner. The DIGNITY ACT immunizes physicians and pharmacists who act in compliance with its comprehensive procedures from civil or criminal sanctions, and any professional disciplinary actions based on that conduct.

The DIGNITY ACT also requires healthcare providers to file reports with the State documenting their actions, thus, Oregon's experience with legal physician-assisted dying has been extensively documented and studied. To date, the Oregon Health Division and/or the Oregon Department of Human Service Office of Disease Prevention and Epidemiology have issued eight annual reports that present and evaluate the state's experience with the DIGNITY ACT. Related reports and articles have also been published in leadings medical journals. These reports constitute the only actual source of reliable data regarding the experience of legal, regulated physician-assisted dying in America.

Predictions of Abuse Unfounded

These reports have shown the dire predictions of those initially opposed to the DIGNITY ACT to be baseless. The data clearly demonstrate that the option of physician-assisted dying has not been unwillingly forced upon those who are poor, uneducated, uninsured or otherwise disadvantaged. The Reports show the following:

- use of physician-assisted dying is strongly associated with a higher level of education; those with a baccalaureate degree or higher were 7.6 times more likely than those without a high school diploma to choose physician-assisted dying.

- ninety-nine percent of patients opting for physician-assisted dying during the DIGNITY ACT's first six years had some form of health insurance and eighty-six percent were enrolled in hospice care.

- use of physician-assisted dying is limited. During the first six years in which physician-assisted dying was a legal option, a total of only 171 Oregonians chose it. The number of terminally ill adults choosing this option in 2003 represented only one-seventh of one percent—i.e., 0.0014 percent—of Oregonians who died that year.

Indeed, rather than posing a risk to patients or the medical profession, the DIGNITY ACT has galvanized significant improvements in the care of the dying in Oregon. These include:

- greatly increased enrollment by Oregon physicians in Continuing Education courses to improve their knowledge of the use of pain medications for the terminally ill, improving their ability to recognize depression and other psychiatric disorders, and more frequently referring their patients to hospice programs.

In sum, the available data demonstrate that making the option of assisted dying available, far from posing any hazard to patients or the practice of medicine, has galvanized improvements in end of life care, benefiting all terminally ill Oregonians.

It's Not about Pain, It's about Loss of Autonomy

The experience in Oregon reveals much about *why* dying patients choose to hasten impending death. In nearly all cases, multiple concerns contributed to the request. The patient's most frequently cited concerns include a decreasing ability to participate in activities that made life enjoyable, the loss of autonomy, and the loss of dignity.

A core argument made in opposition to legalizing the option of assisted dying contends that what terminally ill patients really need is good pain management and palliative care, not hastened death. These opponents contend that motivation to improve pain management will be undermined if assisted dying is an available option. Yet, as noted above, the Oregon experience has shown that legalization of assisted dying has galvanized efforts to *improve* pain management, and hospice enrollment in Oregon is stunningly high among patients who choose to make use of the DIGNITY ACT. Terminally ill Oregonians do not choose assisted dying because they have untreated pain, quite the contrary; Oregonians have access to good pain and symptom management. Only the relatively few patients who find that the cumulative burden of their terminal illness is intolerable, and who persist in a desire to hasten impending death, go on to utilize the DIGNITY ACT.

Doctors and the Public Support Option to Choose

Though Oregon is the only state to have yet legalized the option of physician aid in dying, support for the option is widespread nationwide.

- A Harris poll, January 2002, found that sixty-five percent of respondents support legalization of the right to physician-assisted dying and sixty-one percent favored implementation of a version of the DIGNITY ACT in their own state.

- Another group of studies found that between sixty-three and ninety percent of people with a terminal illness support a right to physician-assisted dying and would like to have the option available to them.

- In California, surveys in March 2006 and March 2005 found that 70% of California residents support the idea that "incurably ill patients have the right to ask for and get life-ending medication." An assisted dying measure introduced in the California State Legislature in 2005 has garnered strong support.

- Support is found among persons of diverse religious faiths. Support is also strong among physicians:

- A national survey conducted in March 2005 found that 57% of physicians believe it is ethical for a physician to assist a competent, dying patient hasten death.

- A 2001 survey published by the *Journal of the American Medical Association* found that fifty-one percent of responding physicians in Oregon supported the DIGNITY ACT and legalization of physician-assisted dying.

- A nationwide survey published in 2001 in the *Journal of General Internal Medicine* found that forty-five percent of responding physicians believed that physician-assisted suicide should be legal, whereas only thirty-four percent expressed views to the contrary.

- Mental health professionals recognize that dying patients can choose aid in dying and be fully mentally competent.

- A significant number of medical associations have decided to embrace a position of "studied neutrality" on the question of legalizing physician-assisted dying, recognizing the division within the medical community on the question.

Without Legal Option, People Tragically Take Matters into Own Hands

Although legal only in Oregon, physicians throughout the country regularly receive requests for assistance in dying. Nearly thirty-percent of physicians responding to a 1998 *New England Journal of Medicine* survey stated that, since entering practice, they had received a request from patients to hasten death. Of those physicians who had received such a request, twenty percent had complied.

A survey of physicians in Washington revealed that twelve percent had received a request to hasten death during the previous year, and twenty-four percent of the patients who requested medications to hasten death received them, notwithstanding the fact that Washington does not have a law in place like the DIGNITY ACT.

Patients who cannot find a physician willing to assist under existing law often act alone or with assistance from family members. Many people shared such stories in amicus briefs submitted to the Supreme Court in the *Glucksberg, Quill* and *OR v. Gonzales* cases. These stories detailed the suffering of loved ones who did not have access or authority to end their own lives. One woman told the story of her husband who had terminal cancer of the spine, lungs, and lymphatic system. Unwilling to await death in a drugged state, her husband kissed

He Wanted to Go When *He* Was Ready

"I know I'm ready," Rick Miller told his doctor over the phone. "I've had Phase 1, and I'm ready for Phase 2." Within two hours, Miller, 52, suffering from terminal cancer, was dead. A bowl of barbiturate-laced applesauce had eased him into a deep and final sleep. Miller's wife of 31 years and their son, Nathan, were at his bedside, holding his hands. His hospice nurse waited outside in the November night. "The last thing he saw was us smiling at him, and he was smiling at us," says Nora Miller, who had watched her husband's lung cancer spread to tumors that riddled his body and eventually confined him to the hospital bed in their Portland, Ore., living room. Days earlier, she had driven to the pharmacy to fill her husband's prescription for 50 Seconal capsules. "He wanted to be able to go," she says, "when he was ready to go."

The dose of barbiturates was not only fatal—it was also legal, prescribed by Miller's doctor and dispensed by a pharmacist under Oregon's 1994 Death With Dignity Act, a unique and fiercely debated experiment in state-sanctioned, physician-assisted suicide.

Liz Halloran, "Of Life and Death,"
U.S. News & World Report, *October 10, 2005.*

his wife good-bye and shot himself in the front yard. "I wish I could have been with him at the end, but he said 'no, it will be messy.'"

Another woman detailed the death of her daughter who was dying of bone cancer. Despite the excruciating pain, her daughter feared for her mother's participation in ending her life. "I should be able to talk with my doctor and plan this, not ask my mom. Mom, what if you go to prison? What will happen to you?" Nonetheless, the woman assisted her daughter by giving her medication. "It was the ultimate act of love a mother could do for her suffering, dying child." When her daughter died, the woman was finally able to hug her daughter without hurting her. Many other such stories have been told: from loved-ones who helped patients die, to others who helplessly watched patients die and the resulting effects on the surviving family members.

Thus, the question is not whether assisted dying will occur, but rather whether it will occur in a regulated and controlled fashion with safeguards and scrutiny, or whether it will occur covertly, in a random, dangerous and unregulated manner.

States Should Allow Assisted Suicide

In *Glucksberg* and *Quill* the Supreme Court recognized that Justice Brandeis's concept of the states as laboratories was particularly applicable to physician assisted dying. The Court's conclusion in those cases that the federal constitution does not bar states from prohibiting physician assisted suicide rested in large part on a reluctance to reach a premature constitutional judgment that would cut off the process of democratic decision-making in the states.

It is timely, prudent and humane for states to enact laws to empower terminally ill, mentally-competent adult citizens to control the timing and manner of their deaths by enabling them to obtain medications from their physician that could be self-administered to bring about a peaceful and humane death, subject to careful procedures. Passage of such laws would harm no one, and would benefit both the relatively few patients in extremis who would make use of them, and a great many more who would draw comfort from knowing this option is available should their dying process become intolerable to them.

| "What looks to some like a choice to die
| begins to look more like a duty to die
| to many disability activists."

Doctor-Assisted Suicide Should Not Be an Option

Diane Coleman

In the following viewpoint, Diane Coleman explains to a U.S. congressional committee why assisted suicide laws are demoralizing and frightening to disabled people and send a harmful message to society. Coleman says, in spite of their physical limitations, disabled people still lead fulfilling, autonomous, and dignified lives. She says the disabled community is worried about assisted suicide laws, like Oregon's, that give physicians—who typically devalue the quality of life of the disabled—the power to decide whether someone's wish to die is rational. Diane Coleman is the executive director of Progress Center for Independent Living, a nonprofit nonresidential service and advocacy center operated by and for people with disabilities.

Diane Coleman, "Testimony before the United States Senate Committee on the Judiciary, Not Dead Yet, The Consequences of Legalized Assisted Suicide and Euthanasia," *Judiciary.senate.gov*, May 25, 2006. Reproduced by permission of the author. Available at http://judiciary.senate.gov/print_testimony.cfm?id=1916&wit_id=5379.

As you read, consider the following questions:

1. According to Coleman, what group provided a legal defense fund to Jack Kevorkian? What happened to the group, and what name does it currently go by?

2. According to Coleman, what are the reasons doctors in Oregon report that they have issued lethal prescriptions? What percentage of the time do they issue a lethal prescription based on a patient's loss of dignity?

3. According to Coleman, where does the state of Oregon rank, when compared to other states, in regard to the number of elderly people who commit suicide?

My name is Diane Coleman. I have a Juris Doctorate and Masters in Business Administration from the University of California at Los Angeles. . . .

I am the Executive Director of Progress Center for Independent Living in Forest Park, Illinois, a nonprofit nonresidential service and advocacy center operated by and for people with disabilities.

I have had a neuromuscular disability since birth, and have used a motorized wheelchair since the age of eleven. From 1987 through 1995, I volunteered as a national organizer for ADAPT, also known as the American Disabled for Attendant Programs Today. I continue to advocate, speak and guest lecture on long-term care issues within Illinois.

When I was six years old, my doctor told my parents that I would not live past the age of 12. A few years later, the diagnosis changed and so did my life expectancy. Over time, I learned that respiratory issues would probably develop. I have friends who've used nighttime ventilators for years, so I knew what symptoms to watch for, and four years ago, started using a breathing machine at night. I had two other friends, one in her 30's and one in her 50's, who needed the same thing. But their doctors discouraged them from it, reinforcing their fears, and either didn't know or didn't disclose what the medical journals said would happen as a result. At an early age, they each went into respiratory distress, and died within a month from infections. A number of my other friends have been pressured by hospital employees to sign do-not-resuscitate orders and other advance directives to forego treatment, coupled with negative statements about how bad it would be if they became more disabled. Frankly, I'm becoming worried about what might happen to me in a hospital if I have a heart attack or other medical crisis. I have appointed my health care proxy, but will the decisions I have entrusted to him be followed by my health care providers? I am not at all convinced that decisions to live are any longer treated with the same respect by health care providers as decisions to die. In fact, I am sure they are not.

Not Dead Yet

Ten years ago, I was on my way to testify before the House Constitution Subcommittee about the opposition to legalized assisted suicide coming from national disability rights organizations. Many of us were worried about Jack Kevorkian, whose body count was 70% people with non-terminal disabilities, and we were worried about two Circuit Courts declaring assisted suicide a constitutional right. Kevorkian even had a legal defense fund provided by the Hemlock Society, later renamed "End-of-Life Choices" and now merged with "Compassion in Dying" to form "Compassion and Choices." In 1996, disability activists had begun to think that we needed a street action group like ADAPT to address the problem, and it was actually the head of ADAPT, Bob Kafka, who thought of our name, taken from a running gag in *Monty Python and The Holy Grail*, "Not Dead Yet." From our viewpoint, assisted suicide laws would create a dangerous double standard for society's response to suicidal expressions, an unequal response depending on one's health or disability status, with physicians as gatekeepers. That sounds like deadly discrimination to us and, frankly, we've been disappointed that the U.S. Dept. of Justice didn't use our civil rights law, the Americans with Disabilities Act, instead of the Controlled Substances Act, to challenge the Oregon assisted suicide law. Like other minority groups, we feel that discrimination is best addressed on the federal level, and states rights have too often meant states wrongs. . . .

Disability rights groups have a unique perspective, informed by both our principles and our experiences. Our principles embrace non-discrimination, civil rights and self-determination. Our collective experiences include monumental struggles against the crushing oppression of a health care system that devalues us and a society that fears significant disability as a fate worse than death. We are consumers on the front lines of the health care system, facing your worst fears with grace and dignity, yet we have been pushed to the margins and even excluded outright from the debate on these issues. . . .

The Real Reason People Ask for Assisted Suicide

Assisted suicide is supposedly about terminal illness, not disability, so many question the legitimacy of disability groups "meddling" and trying to "take away" what they see as the general public's right to choose assisted suicide, some say when they're terminally ill, others say when they're suffering. The stated criteria vary between Compassion and Choices and Final Exit Network, among others, and some people switch group affiliations and eligibility criteria depending on the audience.

The disability experience is that people who are labeled "terminal," based on a medical prediction that they will die within six months, are—or will become—disabled.

The real issue is the reasons people ask for assisted suicide. Although intractable pain has been sold as the primary reason for enacting assisted suicide laws, it's really a "bait-and-switch" situation. The reasons doctors actually report for issuing lethal prescriptions are the patient's "loss of autonomy," "loss of dignity" and "feelings of being a burden."

Those feelings often arise when a person acquires physical impairments that necessitate relying on other people for help in tasks and activities formerly carried out alone. Those are disability issues. In a society that prizes physical ability and stigmatizes impairments, it's no surprise that previously able-bodied people equate disability with loss of dignity.

Studies of patient attitudes toward assisted suicide and euthanasia confirm that "[p]atients' interest in physician-assisted suicide appeared to be more a function of psychological distress and social factors than physical factors." "When patients ask for death to be hastened," another study concluded, "the following areas should be explored: the adequacy of symptom control; difficulties in the patient's relationships with family, friends, and health workers; psychological disturbances, especially grief, depression, anxiety. . . ."

Our Lives Portrayed as Tragedies

The desire for euthanasia or assisted suicide resulted from fear and experience of two main factors: disintegration and loss of community. These factors combined to give participants a perception of loss of self. . . . Symptoms and loss of function can give rise to dependency on others, a situation that was widely perceived as intolerable for participants: "I'm inconveniencing, I'm still inconveniencing other people who look after me and stuff like that. I don't want to be like that. I wouldn't enjoy it, I wouldn't, I wouldn't. No, I'd rather die."

Participants frequently used the notion of dignity to describe the experiences associated with disintegration: . . . "You've become a bag of potatoes to be moved from spot to spot, to be rushed back and forth from the hospital, to be carried to your doctors' appointments or wheeled in a wheelchair, and it really does take away any self-worth, any dignity, or any will to continue to live."

... Loss of community entailed the progressive diminishment of desire and opportunities to initiate and maintain close personal relationships, owing to loss of mobility, exclusion and alienation by others, and self-isolating actions by participants. ...

Participant: "I think we should all be allowed to die with our dignity intact."

Interviewer: "OK and what do you mean by dignity?"

Participant: "Um, the ability to perform simple things like, you know, going to the bathroom on your own and not through a bag, um, breathing with your own lungs, ... I used to be somebody, but now, like I mean, you know, I'm no better than like a doll, somebody has to dress me and feed me and I guess it's uh, I don't know how to explain it, really."

These are common words for newly disabled people.

Disability groups, however, object to the implicit claim that any of us need to die to have dignity.

Needing help in dressing, bathing and other intimate daily tasks does not rob a person of autonomy and dignity. Unfortunately, popular culture has done virtually nothing to educate the public about how people with severe disabilities actually live autonomous and dignified lives. Our lives are portrayed as tragedies or sensationalized as heroism, but the real life issues and coping styles that most people will need if they live long enough are left out of the picture. No wonder people who acquire disabilities so often see death as the only viable solution.

But studies show that whether or not they are terminally ill, people who ask for assisted suicide or euthanasia usually change their minds.

Mistrust of Physicians

The disability rights movement has a long history of healthy skepticism toward medical professionals, and there's an established body of research demonstrating that physicians underrate the quality of life of people with disabilities compared with our own assessments. Our skepticism has grown into outright distrust in our profit-driven health care system.

It should be noted that suicide, as a solitary act, is not illegal in any state. Disability concerns are focused on the systemic implications of adding assisted suicide to the list of "medical treatment options" available to seriously ill and disabled people. The Oregon Law grants civil and criminal immunity to physicians providing lethal prescriptions based on a stated claim of "good faith" belief that the person was terminal, acting voluntarily, and that other statutory criteria were met. This is the lowest culpability standard possible, even below that of "negligence," which is the minimum standard theoretically governing other physician duties.

As the Oregon Reports on physician-assisted suicide make clear, the state has not been able to assess the extent of nonreporting or noncompliance with the law's purported safeguards, but only obtains brief interviews with physicians who file their paperwork. There are no enforcement provisions in the law, and the reports themselves demonstrate that nonterminal people are receiving lethal prescriptions. As the *Oregonian* newspaper stated on March 8, 2005 in "Living with the dying 'experiment,'" examining the case of David E. Prueitt who woke from his assisted suicide after two weeks and did not try again, "The rest of us . . . still need an answer from a system that seems rigged to avoid finding one."

This is the system that controls eligibility for assisted suicide under the Oregon law. Physicians decide who's terminal and who isn't, despite well-known problems with prediction. Physicians decide what "feasible alternatives" to disclose to the individual. I can't help but note, however, that these same doctors have never been required to disclose any financial conflicts of interest they might have in determining what course of treatment to recommend. We're all supposed to take it on faith that no doctor will be influenced by the financial terms of his or her health plan contracts in the information and advice they give. Physicians also decide if the individual's judgment is impaired, if the desire to die seems rational to them.

The Oregon law immunizes physicians from being accountable for each of these decisions.

Oregon Law Gives Physicians Too Much Power

The reasons doctors actually report for issuing lethal prescriptions are the patient's "loss of autonomy" (86%), "less able to engage in activities" (85%), "loss of dignity" (83%), and "feelings of being a burden" (37%). People with disabilities are concerned that these psycho-social factors are being widely accepted as sufficient justification for assisted suicide, with most physicians not even asking for a psychological consultation (14%) or the intervention of a social worker familiar with home and community based services that might alleviate these feelings. The societal message is "so what?" or "who cares?"

The primary underlying practical basis for the physician's determination that the individual is eligible for assisted suicide is the individual's disabilities and physical dependence on others for everyday needs, which is viewed as depriving them of what non-disabled people often associate with "autonomy" and "dignity," and may also lead them to feel like a "burden." This establishes grounds for physicians to treat these individuals completely differently than a physically able-bodied suicidal person would be treated.

In effect, the Oregon Law gives physicians the power to judge whether a particular suicide is "rational" or not based on his or her evaluation, or devaluation, of the individual's quality of life, and then to actively assist certain suicides based on that judgment. The Oregon Death With Dignity Act authorizes and empowers physicians to discriminate in their response to a patient's expression of the wish to die based on the patient's disability. This should be viewed as a violation of the Americans with Disabilities Act, which prohibits such discrimination.

Allowing Assisted Suicide Sends Harmful Message to Society

But perhaps the most important question is not whether the rights of the few people who request assisted suicide and get it have been compromised, though that is a concern, but whether legalizing these individual assisted suicides has a broader social impact. Does it matter that a society accepts the disability-related reasons that people give for assisted suicide, declares the suicide rational and provides the lethal means to complete it neatly? Does it harm people who are not deemed eligible for assisted suicide under the current version of the law, but nevertheless experience severe illnesses and newly acquired disabilities as a loss of dignity and autonomy?

To assess that, I think we should look at the fact that Oregon has the fourth highest elder suicide rate in the country. From the disability rights perspective, this is not surprising. In the face of constant social messages over nearly two decades that needing help in everyday living robs one of dignity and autonomy, makes one a burden and justifies state sponsored suicide, maybe Oregon's elders have taken this disgusting and prejudicial message to heart.

What looks to some like a choice to die begins to look more like a duty to die to many disability activists. I have yet to see an article in which the Oregon health authorities who profess concern about the high rates elder suicide rates go so far as to even mention the Oregon Death With Dignity Act,

A Duty to Die?

The state of Oregon legalized a form of assisted suicide in 1994, but its neighbor to the south, the nation's most populous state, has no such provision. Efforts in California to pass legislation allowing assisted suicide have failed five times over the past fifteen years. California has adopted liberal legislation on any number of controversial issues, but not this one. Why? Assisted suicide proposals have been thwarted by disability rights activists.

The logic of the disability rights movement is easy to understand. Once a society adopts a *right* to die as a matter of policy, a *duty* to die cannot be far behind. This logic is already evident when it comes to babies born with Down syndrome. Among many doctors and ethicists, the question has shifted from the right of parents to abort a baby diagnosed with Down syndrome to a duty to abort.

These doctors and ethicists frame the question this way: What right do you have to bring such a child into this world when we already face huge social costs of health care and face scarce resources? This is the logic of the Culture of Death, but it is a logic now argued rather openly.

Disability rights activists understand that this same logic threatens persons with disabilities. When does the argument for a right to die morph into an argument for a duty to die? The question is not merely a matter of intellectual interest. It is a question of life or death.

Albert Mohler,
"A Threat to the Disabled . . . and to Us All,"
albertmohler.com, *August 2007.*

much less examine the social message behind it. From a disability rights perspective, the potential connection seems obvious. . . .

Listen to Us

To conclude, regardless of our abilities or disabilities, none of us should feel that we have to die to have dignity, that we have to die to be relieved of pain, or that we should die to stop burdening our families or society. Cognitive abilities must not be allowed to determine personhood under the laws of the United States. Reject the script you have been given by the right to die and the right to life movements. Instead, listen to the disability rights movement. We are your advance guard, in anticipation of the aging of our society, with decades of experience in living with disability and on the front lines of the health care system. We offer a very different vision, as well as the practical know-how and leadership to help build a society that respects and welcomes everyone.

"It is ironic and reductive that a tradition that sees a human being as more than her body should give so little weight to existential suffering as a justification for physician assisted suicide."

Doctor-Assisted Suicide Is Not Immoral

Garret Keizer

In the following viewpoint, Garret Keizer contends that the arguments against physician-assisted suicide, particularly moral arguments from the religious right, are disingenuous, unjustified, and flawed. He says the right uses moral arguments in the wrong places. That's why, says Keizer, there can be so much hand-wringing over enabling an elderly woman to die five minutes before "her time." But the decision to invade a country and cause the killing of thousands of innocent children elicits no remorse. He also says the right proclaims to value the sacredness of life, but they reduce the value of life by defining it merely as "being alive." He says allowing physician-assisted suicide won't lead us down a slippery slope. We can allow those terminally ill people who wish to control their destinies the option of assisted suicide

Garret Keizer, "Life Everlasting: The Religious Right and the Right to Die." *Harper's Magazine*, vol. 310, February, 2005, p. 53–61. Copyright © 2005 by Harper's Magazine Foundation. All rights reserved. Reproduced by special permission.

without killing the poor, the elderly, or the disabled who wish to live. Garret Keizer, a former Episcopal priest, is the author of several books.

As you read, consider the following questions:

1. What did Doctor Lloyd Thompson do that got him into trouble, according to Keizer?
2. Keizer says he believes in two moral absolutes. What are they and who first articulated them, according to Keizer?
3. What are the two principles that are central to a liberal society and that according to Keizer, physician-assisted suicide rests upon?

This [is] the ballad of Doctor Lloyd Thompson, who may or may not have hastened a patient's death. This is a song about American secular democracy, which may be under a sentence of death, and about those forces gathering at the gallows. Most of all, this is a song about who owns your life. . . .

Storm over Helping a Patient to Die

The anonymous female patient who made Dr. Thompson known beyond this range of mountains was eighty-five years old, close to death, and, for reasons no one can or will tell me, on a ventilator. Her advance directives had specified that she be kept as comfortable as possible at the end of her life but that no artificial means be employed to prolong it. So either someone at the hospital had suffered a lapse of attention or the woman herself had suffered a lapse in resolve, but in either case we find Dr. Thompson in the position of "weaning" a dying patient off a machine that, in the view of her family, she should not have been on in the first place. After several failed attempts, the patient was at last weaned from the ventilator and given doses of morphine and Versed, standard medications in the palliative procedure known as "terminal sedation." To these drugs Thompson added a third, a neuromuscular blocking agent called Norcuron. The patient died soon thereafter in 2002.

In testimony before the state medical board almost a year later, Thompson conceded that his use of Norcuron had been an error in judgment but insisted that his goal in administering the drug had not been to euthanize the patient but to spare her and her family needless distress should she have regained consciousness. Thompson had treated the patient for twenty years. "She was my friend," he would say. He would not speak to me about his patient or the storm that followed her death, but I did interview him on his work for hospice in connection with a book I was writing at the time his case was decided. His comments suggest that whatever his emotional attachment to the woman, his decisions had been determined in part by his attachment to the idea that "fixing suffering is medicine's crucial job, its great heart, the thing we have always done and have forgotten in our technological interest."

After careful deliberation, the state medical board issued a public reprimand of Thompson and placed a year's probation on his medical license. . . .

States Debating Physician-Assisted Suicide

Dr. Thompson was reprimanded at roughly the same time physician-assisted suicide (PAS) became the subject of a heated debate in the Vermont legislature. . . .

The Vermont bill, which died in committee . . . is modeled closely on the Oregon Death with Dignity Act, to date the only legislation allowing for PAS in the nation. (This is not to suggest that PAS occurs only in Oregon; an estimated one in five doctors will receive a request for PAS at least once in his or her career, and 3 to 18 percent will accede. It is not known how many doctors hasten their own death through professional privelege.). . .

To date, two states have rejected laws based on the Oregon model: Maine by referendum and Hawaii by a close vote in the state legislature. The strongest opposition has come from medical societies (such as the AMA, to which only about 30 percent of the nation's doctors belong) and religious groups, both expressing fears that have so far proved unfounded. Since 1998, only 171 people have made use of the law. PAS has not derailed progress toward good palliative care: Oregon remains a national leader in care for the dying, including the liberal use of opiates. Nor has PAS emerged as the lesser of two evils for the disadvantaged. The typical applicant has tended to be white, well educated, and adequately insured.

But the alarms raised in America's ongoing right-to-die debate have always been characterized by a curious selectivity. You will notice, for example, how the fear of playing God operates exclusively on one side of the medical playground. Thus to help a patient end his or her life "prematurely" is playing God, while extending it in ways and under conditions that no God lacking horns and a cloven hoof could ever have intended is the mandate of "our Judeo-Christian heritage" and the Hippocratic oath. Let someone like Dr. Thompson step out of bounds to honor the spirit of his patient's advance directives, and we will be told that he is eroding respect for the medical profession. But in cases involving a medical professional who blatantly ignores such directives, we are reminded that doctors don't always have time to review patient files while making difficult decisions. They're not God, after all. . . .

The Religious Right Doesn't Want You to Escape from Pain

Assuming that one's life might be taken as the most private of all forms of property, one might also assume that the option for assisted suicide would resonate most powerfully with conservatives. But to make that assumption would give too much weight to ideology and too little to the psychology that informs it. The right talks about protecting life and tradition, but on some level—the level, let's say, where someone like Dr. Thompson is held up for derision—it is mostly interested in protecting pain. For two reasons.

The first is theological: the belief that pain holds the meaning of life. Supposedly, and demonstrably, this is a Christian idea, though if Jesus himself had believed it, he would have told the lepers to find meaning in their sores. The fact is, with even a little encouragement, most lepers do. This explains the conundrum so perplexing to the liberal mind: why hard-pressed people can vote against their own interests in support of someone like George W. Bush. How can they not see? In fact, they do see; they see from the same point of view that has led them to believe that the misery of their lives is the foundation of their integrity.

The second reason, which can always be counted on to exploit the first, is political: the belief that pain is fundamental to justice, which makes perfect sense if justice is conceived as nothing more than a system of punishments and rewards. The essence of punishment is pain. Whoever owns pain owns power.

The suicide, the mystic, the woman who seeks an abortion, the cancer patient who smokes a joint (the cancer patient's long-suffering lover who smokes a joint)—all are roundly condemned for their escape from "responsibility" but truly feared for their escape from jurisdiction. It is a fear with a long and traceable history. The Roman emperor Tarquin crucified the bodies of citizens who committed suicide in order to escape his tyranny. When Margaret Sanger began her campaign for birth control, she was accused of permitting women to escape their God-ordained sorrow in bearing children. . . .

It would be a gross distortion to claim that opposition to physician-assisted suicide is all religious, all from the right, or entirely motivated by some twisted need to see people pay their dues in full. But nearly all the organized opposition to PAS, and especially that of groups like National Right to Life, the Family Forum, The Center for American Cultural Renewal, and the Roman Catholic hierarchy, finds common cause in the need to halt a perceived drift toward nihilism and a disrespect for life.

The Right's Moral Deception

Like the religious right, I believe in moral absolutes. At the very least, I believe in two that were articulated some years ago by the theologian Paul Tillich, those being "the absolute concreteness of every situation in which a moral decision is required" and "the command not to treat a person as a thing." Presumably, the latter of these would preclude vitalizing the body of a vegetative person (of which there are at least 15,000 in this country at any given time) by plugging him into a wall like a Mr. Coffee machine, but I may be taking my absolutes too far.

In contrast, the wisdom of the right consists of knowing how to take its absolutes just far enough, which is to say never so far as to relinquish the prerogatives of wealth and power. The achievement amounts to an ethical sleight of hand. You work the trick by shifting the domain of moral absolutes to those areas of life where they least apply. You treat the gray areas of human existence as though they were black and white, the better to disguise one's self-interested smudging of black and white to gray. You erect castles of rectitude on the frontiers of mortality in the hopes that the murder and raping taking place in the town squares can go on undisturbed. You accept the death of a six-year-old child by aerial bombardment or economic sanctions and defend the life of a six-week-old fetus. Think of it as taking the high road in Lilliput.

From that exalted vantage point, consider Dr. Thompson's cavalier disregard for human life. He may have hastened his patient's death by as much as five minutes. Let's be as reckless as he was and say five hours. But should you perchance check a mortality table, you will discover that life expectancy at birth is roughly five years shorter for an African-American baby than for a white baby. This is true for both genders. In the interests of brevity we will not go into the life expectancies of Creoles born downstream from Louisiana power plants or Pacific Islanders born on former nuclear test sites or country kids born in the back hollows of Dr. Thompson's practice.

What I find especially interesting is the way in which the cold-blooded calculation that launches an invasion in which thousands of children suffer and die is imaginatively transferred to decisions seldom undertaken without struggle and seldom concluded without remorse. The woman who deliberates, procrastinates, and prays late into the night over discontinuing her comatose grandmother's life support is reconceived as an inheritance-mongering opportunist, rubbing her fly-like hands together in the expectation of getting granny's insurance policy five minutes and a potential lawsuit sooner. The family doctor who ventures to ask if there are instances when a too-literal adherence to the Hippocratic vow to "do no harm" might in itself be a form of harm is recast as a hypodermic-wielding assassin, making his house calls on apprehensive old ladies with the remorseless efficiency of a cruise missile. . . .

Reducing the Meaning of Life

It is also ironic, at least for the overwhelming majority of the religious right that identifies itself as Christian, that a religion that arguably began as a rabbinical protest against legalism should devolve to another form of legalism, technically called vitalism, which holds that if it's alive, it's a life. No scurrilously rationalist definition of a human being as an "upright featherless biped" or suchlike was ever so reductive. Similarly, it is ironic (and reductive) that a tradition that sees a human being as more than her body should give so little weight to existential suffering as a justification for PAS. Man may be a little lower than the angels, but his capacity for anguish is reckoned as only a little higher than that of raw meat. The typical argument goes: if physical pain were beyond our powers to relieve, that would be one thing, but the "pain" these death with dignity types are talking about is something else. Many of the supposedly competent patients who ask for PAS are actually depressed, and depression is treatable!. . .

The reductionism of the right extends to the meaning of life itself. The defining quality of human life, as I understand it, is relationship. If there is any idea under the sun that is certifiably "Judeo-Christian," that is it. To be authentically pro-life means something more than protecting a life or my life. It means cherishing the lives of those who come after me or who, in the event of a degenerative illness, will need to take care of me: my wife, my kid, my friends, persons whose lives are likely to be shortened by the stresses of prolonging mine.

If a Death with Dignity law comes to referendum in my state, I will vote for it. I do not know if I would ever use it myself. I remain seated through the credits of movies, even those I didn't much like, and after I've finished my drink, I chew the pulp from the lime. I suspect I'll want to stay for the duration. Perhaps I'll not mind terribly if someone offers me a hug.

But the pertinent question here is not what I will do on my deathbed but what I am prepared to permit others to do on their deathbeds—a distinction that the right is notorious for trying to blur—and on that question I am clear. . . .

We Are Owners of Our Own Lives

PAS rests on two principles that are central to a liberal society.

The first is that we are owners of our own lives. That there is a well-defined domain, roughly coextensive with the boundaries of our own flesh, where we are permitted to have control issues. Permitted, but not obliged—and sometimes, it seems,

Culture of Life or Death?

The religious conservatives do not value actual human life; they are consistent followers of the Christian ideal that human life is properly lived in sacrifice to a supernatural being, and that suffering is proof of virtue. The worship of suffering is fundamental to Christianity, a religion whose central figure is glorified for dying a horrific death for the sins of mankind. Several years ago, a prominent religious conservative said of the Schiavo case, "Terry Schiavo. . .is suffering in obedience to God's will." He added: "Isn't suffering in pursuit of God's will the exact center of religious life?"

This is the culture of death—of living death.

Human life is sacred—not because of supernatural declaration, but because of the unique nature and glorious potential of the individual, rational human life: to think, to create, to love, to experience pleasure, to achieve happiness here on earth. A genuine culture of life would leave individuals free to pursue their own happiness—free from coercive injunctions to sacrifice themselves to religious dogma. Such a culture is what we must seek to create, as we do everything possible to fight religious conservatives' culture of living death.

Alex Epstein, "The Religious Right's Culture of Living Death," Coeur d' Alene Press, *April 22, 2007. Available at www.aynrand.org.*

not even inclined. Only 36 percent of Americans have living wills. In regard to death, our attitude toward physicians remains that of a coquette: we expect the doctor to order our dinner for us, reserving the right to complain if we don't like what shows up on our plate. Or to leave him alone and in disgrace should he turn out to have ordered something not on the menu of "acceptable medical practice."

The second principle, without which liberal individualism always devolves into preciousness, is that we are collective owners of the culture we produce collectively. The debate over PAS is not fundamentally about the Hippocratic oath or the Ten Commandments; it is about who owns the medicine. We continue to behave as though doctors invented, patented, and produced every pill they dispense. I believe doctors are the natural custodians of medicine; I do not believe that custodianship trumps citizenship—especially when a citizen grows too frail to harm anyone but herself or even to help herself, though she may know exactly how she wishes to be helped.

We Are Free to Change Our Minds

And one thing more regarding the relevance of a Death with Dignity law to our democracy: we are free to try it out. We are free to take a step in that direction and then to rescind or expand the step. We are in fact free to do almost anything we wish—except to avoid the issue or deny the freedom. We stand in a place of aches and wonders, with few discernible absolutes besides the necessity to choose and our evolving conviction that it is wrong to use a person as a thing. We can dare to walk on this ground of dubious footing, because we are holding one another up as best we can, and because it is we ourselves and not some deterministic logic that writes our civil laws. We can permit free speech and prosecute libel. We can maintain a military and foreswear militarism. We can, with all due respect to ethicists who claim we can do no such thing, allow abortion and disallow infanticide, and we can do so for the simple reason that it seems like the best thing to do. We can sniff out our options and pick and choose among them, a birthright generally less appreciated by a dogmatist than by a dog.

"You are gods," says one of the Psalms, adding that we shall all die anyway. Perhaps our best defense against the dangers of playing God (chief among them being a death less merciful than we allow to dogs), as well as our best hope of a compromise with those who would adorn our public squares with scriptures graven on tablets of stone, is to sing that verse as though we truly believed it, not in the blind credulity of any fundamentalism but with an intelligence approaching faith.

> *"Here we see the greatest problem with opening the door to suicide as an answer to the problem of suffering caused by illness. Once the law states that assisted suicide is right, the people's own values may soon follow—opening the door to a fall off the vertical moral cliff."*

Doctor-Assisted Suicide Is Immoral

Wesley J. Smith

In the following viewpoint, Wesley J. Smith argues that assisted suicide is wrong because it devalues human life, and it leads society down a slippery slope to a place where killing is seen as an acceptable solution to a myriad number of problems. Smith uses the experience of the Netherlands, a western European country that allows assisted suicide and euthanasia, to illustrate his point. He says the practices of assisted suicide and euthanasia in the Netherlands have changed Dutch values and diminished the morality of the entire country, Wesley J. Smith is an author, a senior fellow at the Discovery Institute, and an attorney for the International Task Force on Euthanasia and Assisted Suicide.

Wesley J. Smith, "Testimony Before the California Senate Judiciary Committee," *www .DiscoveryInstitute.org*, June 20, 2006. Reproduced by permission of the author. Available at www.discovery.org/scripts/viewDB/index.php?command=view&id=3619.

As you read, consider the following questions:

1. According to Smith, how many years before his death was Mr. Freeland issued a lethal prescription?
2. According to Smith, the Dutch have permitted assisted suicide and euthanasia since when?
3. What number of Dutch patients does Smith say are involuntarily euthanized by their doctors each year?

There are two intellectual pillars that proponents argue justify legalizing assisted suicide. The first is an assertion of a near-absolute right of personal autonomy. Accordingly, promoters of assisted suicide generally believe that "the individual's right to self-determination—to control the time, place, and manner of death"—is a paramount liberty interest. The second ideological foundation of assisted suicide advocacy is the belief that killing (ending life) can be an acceptable answer to the problem of human suffering.

Advocacy for legalizing assisted suicide in this country is usually couched in terms that would limit access to those who are terminally ill. But given the philosophical/ideological principles that underlie the assisted suicide movement—that autonomy is paramount and ending life is a valid answer to human suffering—restricting assisted suicide to the dying becomes utterly illogical. After all, many people experience far greater suffering and for a far longer period than people who are terminally ill. Thus, should the two fundamental premises of assisted suicide advocacy become generally accepted by a broad swath of the medical professions and among the public, there is little chance eligibility for "permitted" suicide would long remain limited to the terminally ill.

This isn't a process that would happen instantaneously. The belief in the intrinsic importance of human life is too deeply ingrained within our culture to collapse overnight. But the sheer power of logic may be one of the most irresistible forces in human affairs. Over time, a state sanctioned right of doctors or others to knowingly participate in the suicides or mercy killings of suffering people would lead inexorably to a broader application of hastened death and a steady erosion of the essential principle that each and every human life has equal moral value. . . .

Assisted Suicide Could Be Viewed As Way to Save Money

Arguments in favor of assisted suicide almost always depict the act as occurring in an idealized world that *does not exist*. We are told to presume that decisions to commit assisted suicide would take place in the bosoms of loving families, that suicides would be facilitated by family doctors who have known the patient for decades and are intimately familiar with their values, and that assisted suicide would only be used as a last resort engaged in with great reluctance when nothing else could be done to alleviate unbearable pain.

But this "euthanasia world," as I call it, doesn't exist. There are 7.5 million people without health insurance in [California]—more than the entire population of Oregon—which means almost by definition that they may not have access to quality medical treatment and proper care. The economics of health care are increasingly driven by the HMO in which profits are made by cutting costs, a system which many in this legislature have complained bitterly has resulted in the chipping away of quality care. Some doctors are so stressed by the current system that patients may have a mere 15 minutes or less within which to interact with their doctors.

The cost for the drugs used in assisted suicide is about $50. It could take $500,000 to provide the patient with proper care so they don't want assisted suicide. Should assisted suicide become legalized and legitimized, the economic force of gravity is obvious. After all, what could be a "cheaper" medical treatment than hastened death?

Perhaps that is why you don't see poor people demonstrating in the streets or demanding the right to assisted suicide: They are worried about receiving adequate care!. . .

Meanwhile, many of our families are under increasing strain. Debt is at an all time high, and elder abuse is rampant. The temptation that would be posed by inheritance and life insurance when families pondered whether to support a family member's request for assisted suicide is obvious. And think about how the despair caused by the all too frequent neglect of our seniors and disabled people—too many of whom languish abandoned in nursing homes and other care facilities—could affect a decision to seek a poison prescription when deciding whether to support the legalization of hastened death.

Assisted suicide would be wrong even under the most ideal conditions. But in light of these stark realities, and considering the frayed safety net . . . , legalizing assisted suicide . . . could have catastrophic consequences for the weak, vulnerable, depressed, and unwanted.

Eventually, assisted suicide could come to be seen as a splendid way to save scarce medical resources. . . .

Guidelines Will Not Protect Against Abuse

The usual response to such concerns by assisted suicide advocates is the blithe assurance that "strict guidelines will protect against abuse." At best, this is extremely naïve. Once we create classes of people whose suicides the state's public policy states can be legally facilitated, it is easy for these people's lives to come to be perceived as [being] less valuable than those who are required by state policies to receive suicide prevention.

We are told repeatedly that Oregon demonstrates that legalizing assisted suicide is "safe." Yet, elder and youth suicide are acute problems in Oregon and state attempts to prevent suicide are not aided by a law that explicitly validates the suicides of some Oregon residents—sending a clear mixed message to Oregon's suicidal citizens.

But be that as it may, little is truly known about the actual practice of assisted suicide in Oregon since almost all of the information the state garners about what is happening depends on self-reporting by lethally prescribing doctors—who are about as likely to tell the state that they violated the law as they are to tell the IRS they cheated on their taxes. . . .

Mr. Freeland

Still, we know about a few cases of apparent abuse. One of the most disturbing is that of a cancer patient named Michael P. Freeland, who gave permission for his medical records to be reviewed for a peer-reviewed article published in the *Journal of American Psychiatry*. To the best of my knowledge, it is the only case so far in which professional investigators had access to the actual medical records of a patient who received a lethal prescription under Oregon's law.

The authors of the study, psychiatrist N. Gregory Hamilton and Catherine Hamilton, a social worker, discovered that "Mr. A." (Freeland), had been issued a lethal prescription nearly *2 years* before he actually died of natural causes. (Dr. Hamilton is the former president of Physicians for Compassionate Care, an organization dedicated to improving palliative care for the dying, but which also opposes Oregon's law. He and Catherine Hamilton are married.) This is a matter of striking interest. Not only was Freeland apparently not terminally ill as defined by Oregon's law (which requires that a doctor reasonably believe that a patient will die within 6 months) when he first received his lethal prescription, but even more alarmingly, he was allowed to keep his cache of suicide pills even after being diagnosed as having "depressive disorder," "chronic adjustment disorder with depressed mood," "intermittent delirium," for which he was hospitalized and declared mentally incompetent by a court.

Here are the details: Mr. Freeland was diagnosed with lung cancer in 2000. In early 2001 he received a lethal prescription from Dr. Peter Reagan, an assisted suicide advocate who is often referred patients whose own doctors refuse to assist the suicides of their patients. On January 23, 2002, more than a year after receiving Reagan's lethal script, Freeland was admitted to a hospital psychiatric ward for depression with suicidal and possibly homicidal thoughts. A social worker went to Freeland's home and found it "uninhabitable," with "heaps of clutter, rodent feces, ashes extending two feet from the fireplace into the living room, lack of food and heat, etc. Thirty-two firearms and thousands of rounds of ammunition were removed by the police." Amazingly, the "lethal medications" that had been prescribed more than a year before were left in the house.

Freeland was hospitalized for a week and then discharged on January 30. The discharging psychiatrist noted with approval that his guns had been removed, "which resolves the major safety issue," but wrote that Freeland's lethal prescription remained "safely at home." Freeland was permitted to keep the overdose even though the psychiatrist reported he would "remain vulnerable to periods of delirium." In-home care was considered likely to assist with this problem, but a January 24 chart notation noted that Freeman "does have his life-ending medications that he states he may or may not use, so that [in-home care] may or may not be a moot point."

It was during this period that Freeland called Physicians for Compassionate Care for help. Rather than dying alone by assisted suicide, he was instead cared for by the Hamiltons and by his friends—who assured the now imminently dying man "that they valued him and did not want him to kill himself." Freeland was properly treated for depression with medication. He received good pain control, including a morphine pump. Best of all, he was reunited with his estranged daughter and died knowing she loved him and would cherish his memory.

His Life Had Lesser Value

Based on their review of the facts and circumstances surrounding Freeland receiving a lethal prescription and being allowed to keep the drugs while psychotic, the Hamiltons reached important conclusions about the law's discriminatory effect on patients and its impact on mental health professionals:

> The legalization of doctor-assisted suicide in Oregon has resulted in the introduction of competing paradigms—the traditional clinical approach [Removing lethal means is central to the clinical treatment of suicide symptoms] and the assisted suicide competency model [providing lethal means]—for responding to suicidal thoughts and behaviors in seriously ill individuals.... These competing models appear to be based on incompatible underlying assumptions about the value of protecting life depending on predictions of how long a patient might live.... We conclude that the attempt to mix models is confusing to both clinicians and patients and endangers seriously ill patients, particularly those with a history of pre-existing mental illness.

Or to put it another way, the very mental health professionals responsible for treating this delusional man expressed utter indifference to his committing suicide, whereas had he presented the same symptoms without having cancer he would undoubtedly have received rigorous suicide prevention and treatment. The only conclusion to draw from such a disparity is that because he had obtained a suicide prescription, the value of Mr. Freeland's life was perceived to be of lesser value to his own psychiatrist. . . .

The Dutch Experience

We need only look to the experience of the Netherlands to see . . . the destructive social forces that assisted suicide ideology unleashes. The Dutch have permitted euthanasia and assisted suicide since 1973. Euthanasia and assisted suicide became an integral part of Dutch medicine after a court ruling that refused to meaningfully punish a physician, Geetruida Postma, who had euthanized her mother. The court accepted the premise—supported by both the prosecution and the defense—that most Dutch doctors favored euthanasia in some cases. Accordingly, even though convicted of murder, Dr. Postma received only a one-week suspended sentence and a year's probation.

Other court decisions soon followed, with each widening and further liberalizing the conditions under which euthanasia and assisted suicide would not be punished. Thus, even though these life-terminating practices remained technically illegal until 2002, they became deeply entrenched in Dutch medical practice. At this point it is important to recall that when euthanasia was first accepted in the Netherlands, it was supposed to be a rare event, to be resorted to only in the most unusual cases of "intolerable suffering." . . . The guidelines were designed specifically to keep assisted suicide occurrences few and far between by establishing demanding conditions that had to be met, at the risk of criminal prosecution. Over time, however—precisely *because* suicide and mercy killing were deemed acceptable answers to human suffering—doctors began to interpret the death regulations loosely and even ignore them altogether. In the few circumstances where the law took notice, the courts accommodated expanded euthanasia through continual loosening of the meaning of the guidelines. . . .

Assisted Suicide Alters the Concept of Right and Wrong

But the issue goes much deeper than doctors refusing to obey and law enforcement authorities refusing to enforce the rules. What euthanasia really did to the Dutch was to profoundly alter the nation's conception of right and wrong. With the widespread acceptance of assisted suicide consciousness in the

Netherlands, the guideline limitations became mere window dressing that made little actual difference at the bedside to doctors or, indeed, to much of the general public. Finding the proverbial exception to the rule became a standard practice, which in turn, soon changed the exception into the rule. The official guidelines then expanded to formally authorize what was already being done.

The words of the late physician, Dr. K.F. Gunning, perhaps the most notable Dutch opponent of euthanasia, need to be heeded: "Once you accept killing as a solution for a single problem, you will find tomorrow hundreds of problems for which killing can be seen as a solution." And indeed, since 1973 Dutch doctors have gone from killing the terminally ill who ask for it, to the chronically ill who ask for it, to the disabled who ask for it, to depressed people who aren't even physically ill who ask for it. . . .

Killing Babies and Those Who Have Not Asked

Perhaps the clearest indication of how assisted suicide and euthanasia affects our perceptions of the value of human life can be seen in the non voluntary mercy killings that permeate Dutch euthanasia practice.

In the Netherlands, infants are killed because they have birth defects, and doctors justify the practice. A 1997 study published in the British medical journal, *The Lancet*, revealed how deeply pediatric euthanasia had metastasized into Dutch neonatal medical practice. According to the report, doctors killed approximately 8 percent of all infants who died in the Netherlands in 1995. Assuming this to be typical, this amounts to approximately 80–90 infanticides per year. Of these, one-third would have lived more than a month. At least 10–15 of these killings involve infants who did not depend on life-sustaining treatment to stay alive. The study found that 45 percent of neo-natologists and 31 percent of pediatricians, who responded to study's questionnaires, had killed infants. A follow up study of end-of-life decisions made for infants published in the April 9, 2005 issue found that nothing had changed. . . .

In 2004, Groningen University Medical Center made international headlines when it admitted to permitting pediatric euthanasia and published the "Groningen Protocol," infanticide guidelines the hospital had utilized when killing 15–20 disabled newborns. The Protocol creates three categories of killable infants: infants "with no chance of survival," infants with a "poor prognosis and are dependent on intensive care," and "infants with a hopeless prognosis," including those "not depending on intensive medical treatment but for whom a very poor quality of life . . . is predicted."

In addition to killing babies, Dutch doctors routinely euthanize patients who have not asked to die. Repeated studies demonstrate that each year at least 900–1000 Dutch patients are non-voluntarily euthanized by their doctors. The practice even has a name, "termination without request or consent," and even though this is formally considered murder under Dutch law, it is rarely prosecuted and almost never meaningfully punished.

Making matters worse . . . despite the clear abuses in the Netherlands, despite the uncontestable fact that doctors are now euthanizing babies and people who have not asked to be killed—the Dutch people support their country's euthanasia policy. And here we see the greatest problem with opening the door to suicide as an answer to the problem of suffering caused by illness. Once the law states that assisted suicide is right, the people's own values may soon follow—opening the door to a fall off of the vertical moral cliff.

The Slippery Slope Is Real

Based on the above, what can we conclude? First, the slippery slope is very real. The Dutch have proved that Dr. Gunning

Suffering Has Value

To the insensitive eye, my patient looked healthy, not particularly distressed or anxious. He had no pain or difficulty breathing. He was recovering and could expect to return to a productive life. Yet he found his life unbearable, and wanted to be done with it.

Perhaps others might have felt compelled, even obligated, to help him end his life. When suffering, moral or physical, is relentless and overwhelming, ending it all might seem like the merciful thing to do.

But I can't help feeling that mercy of this sort is misguided.

To advocate physician-assisted suicide is to deny that human suffering has value, and to affirm that the absence of things unpleasant is a necessary condition for a life worth living.

Jose A. Bufill,
"An Assisted Suicide Kills More Than One Person,"
Nightingale Alliance, *June 24, 2004.*

was right; once killing is accepted as a solution for one problem, tomorrow it will be seen as the solution for hundreds of problems. Once we accept the assisted suicide of terminally ill patients, we will—over time—come to accept the killing of chronically ill patients, disabled people, depressed patients, and ultimately perhaps, even children. Indeed, we saw this slippery slope phenomenon during the assisted suicide spree of Jack Kevorkian, in which more than 70% of the people he assisted in suicide were not terminally ill—and five weren't even ill upon autopsy.

Second, adopting suicide as an acceptable answer to human suffering eventually changes popular outlooks. The law not only reflects our values, but in our diverse age, it tells us right from wrong. Accordingly, once suicide is redefined as medical treatment, it becomes transformed from "bad" into "good." Thus, the guidelines intended to "protect against abuse" eventually are viewed not as protections but instead as hurtles separating sick and dying patients from the beneficence of death. In such an intellectual and cultural milieu, it becomes easy to justify ignoring or violating "guidelines."

Third, legalizing assisted suicide can distort the attitude of medical professionals toward their sickest patients. This would be especially true in a medical economic system dominated by cost containment and managed care where profits come from reducing the level of services.

Fourth, legalizing assisted suicide sends the implied message that people who are diagnosed with a terminal illness have lives less worthy of being protected than those of other suicidal people. I have seen this very paradigm in action as a hospice volunteer.

Robert Salamanca of Pleasanton was a wonderful friend who I met as hospice volunteer when he was dying of Lou Geherig's disease. Bob believed strongly that assisted suicide advocacy diminished the value of the lives of people like him. Indeed, he felt so strongly about this he wrote an important op/ed column in the *San Francisco Chronicle* (while completely paralyzed) which stated in part:

> Euthanasia advocates believe they are doing people like me a favor. They are not. The negative emotions toward the terminally ill and disabled generated by their advocacy is actually at the expense of the 'dying' and their families and friends, who often feel disheartened and without self assurance because of a false picture of what it is like to die created by these enthusiasts who prey on the misinformed.
>
> What we, the terminally ill, need is exactly the opposite—to realize how important our lives are. And our loved ones,

friends, and indeed society, need to help us feel that we are loved and appreciated unconditionally.

Robert was right. The proper approach to death and dying is to increase our levels of care and compassion, not permit doctors to coolly write lethal prescriptions.

> *"To be a true proponent of life, one has to affirm all of life—and that means not only helping people to live fully but also to die well."*

Palliative Care Should Be Considered Instead of Assisted Suicide

Ira Byock

In the following viewpoint, Ira Byock says that hospice and palliative care helps people to die well. Hospice and palliative care accepts that death is inevitable, but does not hasten it. The focus is on relieving the suffering of terminally ill patients rather than trying to cure them. Byock says that, as a proponent of hospice and palliative care, he is often attacked by the extreme right that believes death should be fought in every circumstance and at any cost. This group opposes "do-not-resuscitate" orders and removal of feeding tubes. On the other end of the spectrum, says Byock, he is accused of having a religious agenda because he does not believe death should be hastened. Byock says palliative care does not fight death nor reach for it, but allows it to come in the most

Ira Byock, "To Life! Reflections on Spirituality, Pallative Practice and Politics," *American Journal of Hospice & Palliative Medicine*, vol. 23, January, 2007, p. 436–438. Copyright © 2007 Sage Publications. Republished with permission of Sage Publications, Inc.

meaningful, human, and spiritual way possible. Ira Byock is an author, professor, and the director of palliative care at Dartmouth Medical School and the director and co-founder of the Reclaiming the End of Life Initiative.

As you read, consider the following questions:

1. According to Byock, how does existentialism see the universe?
2. What does *La Chaichim* mean?
3. According to Byock, opposing testimony on New Hampshire HB 656 from the far Right made it seem as if death was always what? What does Byock say death is?

D riving home from the medical center through spring rain on a dreary Sunday afternoon, I was struck, once again, by the stunning beauty and imperfect perfection of the world. There was something within the wet shades of green and brown of the trees and forest loam. There was life, hunkered and healthy within the gloom.

Weekends are quieter at the hospital and rounds that day mostly comprised sitting with people who were approaching the ends of lengthy illnesses. Somehow, in every room, we wound up talking about life.

Love Outlasts Death

Alice (not her real name) was a 47-year-old woman with advanced intraperitoneal [within the abdomen] cancer and ascites [excess fluid] who was admitted the previous week when her leg suddenly turned cold and blue. After the successful removal of an arterial clot restored circulation to the limb, she developed kidney failure. When I visited Alice in her hospital room, after the requisite pain and bowel update, we indulged in musings about illness, healing, God, and love. The conversation began when I asked about the collection of [thirteenth century Persian] Rumi poems on her bedside table. We read a few and then I shared a favorite poem and asked her to guess who wrote it.

You do not need to leave your
room,
Remain sitting at your table and
listen.
Do not even listen, simply wait.
Do not even wait, be quiet still and
solitary.
The world will freely offer itself to
you to be unmasked.
It has no choice.
It will roll in ecstasy at your feet.

She correctly surmised it wasn't Rumi, but was surprised to learn the poet was Franz Kafka, the quintessential existential-ist. Existentialism sees the universe as cold and impersonal, leaving each individual exposed to circumstance and happen-stance, ultimately reliant only on him or herself. Yet Kafka rec-ognized an esthetic intelligence within the very stuff of reality. This led Alice and me to talk about chaos theory, fractals, pat-terns within randomness, and of God within us all and all that is. She spoke about healing and well-being in the face of loss.

Alice's husband arrived from their home in time to wit-ness, bemused, the crescendo of this brief reverie. Knowing from our previous discussions the remarkable story of their mid-life romance, 3-year marriage, and expanding love through her illness, I said that I've come to believe that love is stronger than death. For one thing, love outlasts death to live on within others. But the love of 2 people can also be a fiercely defiant act, for love affirms life in the face of death. Looking though my windshield and the rain that day, I had the image in my mind of Alice and her husband holding hands, beaming into each other's eyes.

Palliative Care Reveres Life and Spirituality

Mortality teaches us a lot about life, if we let it. One thing it teaches is that human life is inherently spiritual, whether or not a person has a religion. Recently, I asked a gruff elderly Vermont farmer, whom I saw in clinic, whether he had a sense of what comes after this life. He chuckled and replied, "The worms go in; the worms go out."

Half-expecting such a response, I asked. "And where will the worms go in and out of *your* bones?"

"Oh, we have a family cemetery on a hill in Thetford. We Gradys (not his real name) have been buried there for over a century and I suspect my grandchildren and their grandchildren will be there, too."

Mr. Grady doesn't pray, attend church, or believe in God, but he has a strong sense of connection to the land and to his family, ancestors who preceded him and relatives who will be born into generations to come. The meaning and value he derives from being part of something that is larger and more enduring than his own life seems authentically, unassumingly spiritual to me.

In fact, the confrontation with death lays bare the spiritual core of the human condition. Human spirituality arises in response to the awe-inspiring and terrifying mystery of life and the universe. We reflexively seek to make meaning of our experience in the world and make or strengthen our connections to others.

Hospice and palliative care clinicians recognize this anthropologic truth. Reverence for life resonates within our field and we are generally recognized for attending to these inherently human dimensions of suffering and well-being.

Hospice Attacked by Right to Death and Right to Life Groups

Yet we live and practice in nonordinary times. And not everyone trusts our motives or approves of our practices.

What Hospice Is About

[Hospice] is about an end-of-life option meant to bring comfort, dignity, calm and order.

It is also about letting the person know he or she has some choices and control in facing this letting-go.

Its underlying precepts can be summarized this way:

- Death is a natural part of life, and when it is inevitable, hospice will neither hasten it nor postpone it.

- Death is both a physical and spiritual experience.

- Hospice establishes pain and symptom control.

- Loved ones and friends are part of the program.

- Bereavement care is critical to the family and friends left behind.

- Hospice care is made available by most hospice programs, regardless of the patient's ability to pay.

- Hospice can be anywhere: a nursing home, inpatient units, one's own home or a designated hospice residence.

Hospice teams bring a deep sense of compassion, expert knowledge, and respect for the dignity and wisdom of each individual as he or she encounters death in his or her own way.

No less a benefit is the peace of mind that comes with the dying person knowing that he or she has been made to feel as comfortable as possible, and the peace of mind that loved ones get by knowing such care is taking place.

Susan Abbott, "We Should Give Life to Those We Serve,"
Assisted Living, *August, 2007.*

On one end of the spectrum, a few ardent proponents of legalizing physician-assisted suicide accuse us of forcing people to suffer by refusing to prescribe lethal medications. Recently an elderly physician committed (unassisted) suicide in an assisted-living center in the Upper Connecticut Valley. I was called by a reporter to comment on the phenomenon of elder suicides and was subsequently quoted in a local newspaper saying that it seems tragic when someone of any age feels that life is not worth living and takes his or her own life. The next day a reader sent an e-mail suggesting that I, and my colleagues in palliative care, secretly harbor a religious agenda.

Interesting thought. I don't think of myself as religious. But in full disclosure, I was raised by Jewish parents, and although I am not particularly observant of holidays or rituals, my sense of the inherent value of life has roots deep within my ancestry and upbringing. Life is an absolute value for Jews. Many Jews wear the Hebrew symbol for life, *Chai* as pendants around their necks. We toast *La Chaichim!* (to life) as we raise glasses in celebration. If reverence for life constitutes a religious agenda, I suppose I have one.

On the other extreme, a fringe element of the right-to-life movement regularly accuses hospice, palliative care, and even intensivists of killing innocent victims each time we write or honor a do-not-resuscitate (DNR) order or permit a person to die without a feeding tube. Think I'm exaggerating? Consider the recent saga of New Hampshire House Bill 656.

The bill began in 2004 as a prosaic effort by concerned citizens to update the state's advance directive law, removing the antiquated requirement to have the document signed in front of a notary public and creating a consistent way for emergency medical technicians to honor DNR orders outside of hospitals. But in the wake of Terri Schiavo's death, the far Right hijacked the bill for political purposes. They inserted statutory language requiring anyone without an advance directive to undergo medically administered nutrition and hydration and cardiopulmonary resuscitation (CPR) before death. These provisions were designed to be symbolically potent and inflammatory, but they made no biologic sense and, therefore, no legal sense.

Respectful efforts by the citizens committee who had crafted the original bill to explain the pragmatically and medically troubling aspects of the proposed requirements and reach a constructive understanding were ignored or turned aside. In hearings in both chambers of the New Hampshire legislature, I and other medical professionals testified that, while we agreed with the presumption of performing CPR in most circumstances, exemptions were needed for situations in which death is imminent and CPR is not medically indicated or would cause unnecessary harm. Similarly, while accepting the presumption of sustaining life through medically administered nutrition and hydration, we extended an amendment encompassing situations, such as advanced, multisystem failure, in which persisting in administering intravenous or enteral nutrients would cause unnecessary suffering or hasten a patient's death.

Opposing testimony from the far Right made it seem as if death was always optional, in each case the result of a doctor's DNR order or an alleged decision "to starve an innocent victim," rather than the inevitable consequence of aging, diseases, or injuries. . . .

Thankfully, the Senate Judiciary Committee later reinstated rational exemptions which permit clinicians to discontinue artificial nutrition and hydration when it would hasten death or cause suffering and to write DNR orders when death was expected or efforts to resuscitate a person would be useless and merely cause harm. After contentious debates and rancorous parliamentary maneuvering, the bill was passed and signed into law with those provisions intact. A crisis was averted, but an acrimonious cultural chasm remains.

Having stood personally with faith-based organizations, including fundamentalist Christian groups, in opposing proposals to legalize physician-assisted suicide, this all feels highly ironic and disheartening. The uncivil war over abortion has long threatened to engulf rational debate over assisted suicide, and by extension, polarize any discussion of how we die. Still, I have always thought that providing medically excellent, unabashedly tender, loving care was bedrock common ground—a tangible expression of the values that unite people on the far Left and the far Right. Apparently, I was naïve. On the Internet and, indeed, on the floor of the New Hampshire legislature, doctors who allow people to die without inflicting unwanted or useless medical treatments are accused of promoting a "culture of death." The practices they decry are epitomized by hospice and palliative care.

Dying Well

These invectives are couched in the name of religion, but they have nothing to do with authentic religious teaching. Although I was raised Jewish, I've often been well guided in my practice by the teachings of other great religions, including Catholicism. In his final months, the late Chicago Cardinal Bernadin wrote an open letter to the Supreme Court opposing the legalization of physician-assisted suicide. He observed:

> I am at the end of my earthly life. There is much that I have contemplated these last few months of my illness, but as one who is dying I have especially come to appreciate the gift of life. I know from my own experience that patients often face difficult and deeply personal decisions about their care. However, I also know that even a person who decides to forgo treatment does not necessarily choose death. Rather, he chooses life without the burden of disproportionate medical intervention.

Cardinal Bernardin's words do not express a culture of death but, rather, describe the proper relationship of medical treatment to human life. Whatever our politics, clinicians who practice hospice and palliative care comprise the most ardent pro-life group in America. To be a true proponent of life, one has to affirm *all* of life—and that means not only helping people to live fully but also to die well.

> "It seems reasonable to question the policies that universally deny such a basic opportunity [i.e. assisted suicide] to the mentally ill."

People Suffering from Mental Illness Should Be Allowed to Choose Assisted Suicide

Jacob M. Appel

In the following viewpoint, Jacob Appel contends that assisted suicide should be made available to the mentally ill. Appel sees no distinction between the physical suffering of a patient with amyotrophic lateral sclerosis (ALS), a fatal neurodegenerative disease, and the psychological suffering of severe depression, one of the most common mental illnesses. He thinks that prohibiting the mentally ill from accessing assisted suicide is misplaced paternalism. The mentally ill should have more options not less, says Appel. Jacob Appel is a bioethics writer, a lawyer and the author of numerous works of fiction.

Jacob M. Appel, "A Suicide Right for The Mentally Ill? A Swiss Case Opens a New Debate," *Hastings Center Report*, vol. 27, May/June 2007, pp. 21–23. Copyright © 2007 Hastings Center. Reproduced by permission.

As you read, consider the following questions:

1. According to Appel, the fifty-three-year-old manic depressive who took his case to the Swiss Supreme Court claimed a right to what? He did so under Article 8 of which European Convention?

2. According to Appel, what are the twin goals at the core of the argument supporting assisted suicide?

3. According to Appel, the most compelling argument against extending assisted suicide rights to the mentally ill relates to the role of whom?

Advocates for the legalization of assisted suicide in the United States, including those who sponsored Oregon's Death with Dignity Act in 1994 and backers of California's proposed Compassionate Choices Act, have sought to permit the practice only under highly limited circumstances—namely, when the requesting patient is terminally ill. In contrast, the Netherlands allows physician-assisted suicide in nonterminal cases of "lasting and unbearable" suffering, and Belgium authorizes physician-assisted suicide for nonterminal patients when their suffering is "constant" and "cannot be alleviated." Yet no country has laws on the subject as liberal as those of Switzerland, where assisted suicide has been legal since 1918. It remains the only jurisdiction that allows nonresidents to terminate their own lives. It is also the only jurisdiction that does not require that a physician be involved in the process.

Swiss Court Rules Assisted Suicide Should Be Available to Mentally Ill

Now, a decision by the Swiss Federal Supreme Court threatens to undermine yet another longstanding taboo in the debate over assisted suicide and euthanasia. In its ruling on November 3, 2006, the high tribunal in Lausanne laid out guidelines under which, for the first time, assisted suicide will be available to psychiatric patients and others with mental illness.

The case was that of an unnamed fifty-three-year-old manic depressive with two prior suicide attempts who sought a prescription for fifteen grams of sodium pentobarbital in order to end his own life. He claimed a right to self-determination under Article 8 of the European Convention on Human Rights and alleged that no physician would prescribe him this lethal dose for fear of legal or professional repercussions. Dignitas, a Zurich-based advocacy group, supported his suit. The Swiss high court responded with a sweeping opinion upholding the right of those suffering from "incurable, permanent, severe psychological disorders" to terminate their own lives. According to the court, a distinction should be made between temporarily impaired individuals who wish to die as "an expression of treatable psychological disturbances" and those individuals with severe, long-term mental illness who have made "rational" and "well-considered" decisions to end their lives to avoid further suffering. Since serious mental disorders could make life seem as unbearable to some patients as serious somatic ailments do to others, the court reasoned, those who repeatedly expressed a wish to end their lives under such circumstances should be permitted to do so. (The court also ruled that the plaintiff in this case would have to obtain a thorough psychiatric evaluation to determine whether he met these standards before he could end his life.)

Principles of Assisted Suicide Extend Logically to Mentally Ill

Both supporters and opponents of assisted suicide have been highly critical of extending suicide rights to psychiatric patients. One set of objections is directed against the practice of assisted suicide itself—for a host of reasons ranging from a belief in the inherent sanctity of human life to a fear of sliding down a slippery slope toward involuntary euthanasia; that debate has been extensively addressed elsewhere. Another set of objections are from those who support a basic right to assisted suicide in certain situations, such as those of terminal disease, but do not wish to extend it to cases of severe and incurable mental illness. This resistance may be inevitable, considering the increased emphasis that contemporary psychiatry places on suicide prevention, but the principles favoring legal assisted suicide lead logically to the extension of these rights to some mentally ill patients.

At the core of the argument supporting assisted suicide are the twin goals of maximizing individual autonomy and minimizing human suffering. Patients, advocates believe, should be able to control the decision of when to end their own lives, and they should be able to avoid unwanted distress, both physical and psychological. While these two principles might explain why a victim of amyotrophic lateral sclerosis or cancer would choose assisted suicide, they apply equally well in many cases of purely psychological disease: a victim of repeated bouts of severe depression, particularly in cases where treatment has consistently proven ineffective, rationally might prefer dignified death over future suffering.

Obviously, there is a difference in kind between the terminally ill cancer patient and the acutely depressed teenager who transiently desires to end his life after a romantic setback; it seems logical to prevent patients from committing suicide until they have considered all of their options over an extended period of time, and to be certain that they are not acting in haste. But the difference between a patient who desires suicide after enduring the long-term agonies of rheumatoid arthritis or trigeminal neuralgia and the patient who wants to end his life after years of debilitating anxiety or intermittent psychotic episodes is not so clear.

One crucial distinction between chronic mental illness and terminal disease is that death is inevitable in the latter cases. Yet "inevitable" is really not quite right. From today's vantage point, a rapid cure for ALS or certain cancers appears highly unlikely, yet the history of modern medicine is replete with examples of illnesses (type I diabetes, acute lymphoblastic leukaemia, choriocarcinoma) that have rapidly gone from universally fatal to highly manageable. What we really mean when we speak of inevitability is that we believe the patient should be able to weigh the unlikely possibility of a cure against her other interests. While the window of opportunity for discovering effective treatment may be longer in cases of chronic mental illness, it seems reasonable to afford the patient the same choice in balancing likelihoods against other values. And if the offer is that an effective treatment may eventually be found, but a person will have to suffer for some decades more until that happens, then it might still be rational to prefer suicide.

Patient Competency and Physician Conflict of Interest

A second concern in cases of mental illness is that of the competence of the decision-maker. For example, a severely depressed patient might substantially underestimate her long-term prognosis. But rather than arguing against assisted suicide, this might indicate even further the depth of the patient's present suffering. Clearly, patients who experience psychosis or are incapable of making general medical decisions should not be able to take their own lives until they can think rationally. Morever, the finality of a life-terminating decision indicates that a higher threshold of competence should be required in suicide cases than in more run-of-the-mill health care choices. But one can be both deeply depressed and capable of making rational decisions. If the values championed by assisted suicide advocates are maximazation of autonomy and minimization of suffering—even when they conflict with the extension of life—then it follows that chronically depressed, competent individuals would be ideal candidates for the procedure. At the very least, a patient with a history of mental illness who is currently experiencing a temporary remission of symptoms will certainly be competent enough to

Everybody Has Right to End Life

The fact that the Swiss Supreme Court has acknowledged the Right to Suicide as a Human Right also makes it clear that, in order to make use of this right, there are no other conditions than capacity of discernment, capacity of expression and capacity to make the last act in one's life.

Therefore one of the results of this decision must be that the debate concerning whether or not somebody who can be granted assisted suicide must be terminally ill—or even ill at all—should be closed.

Human Rights in general apply to every human being without any precondition; the preconditions of capacity of discernment, capacity of expression and capacity to make the last act in one's life are set not in respect to the Human Right to suicide, but to the capacity to commit a suicide assisted by a third party.

So everybody has the right to end his or her life, and the contracting states of the European Convention on Human Rights might have no other duty than to ensure that such decisions are made by informed citizens and are well considered.

Ludwig Minelli, "The Decision of the Swiss Federal Court of November 3, 2006," ALDE Hearing, Dignitas, July 5, 2007.

make such a choice before the return of the disease. (An additional concern might be the increased suffering endured by families of assisted suicide victims—but why this suffering should trump that of the patient is not clear.)

The most compelling argument against extending assisted suicide rights to the mentally ill relates to the role of physicians. The nature of psychiatric therapy differs from that of other medical treatment in the degree of attachment between caregiver and patient. This distinction is recognized in various regulatory codes, and most glaringly in the rules banning romantic relations between psychiatrists and former patients, even many years after care has ceased. Moreover, psychiatrists are trained to prevent suicide—an outcome widely regarded by the profession as a failure. This conflict of interest places the psychiatrist in the unpleasant bind of choosing between a patient's wish and the standard of care in the field. Psychiatrists might even attempt to avoid treating such rational but chronically suicidal patients in an effort to avoid this choice. Any meaningful discussion of the subject of assisted suicide for the mentally ill should include an exploration of alternative mechanisms by which such patients might obtain help in ending their lives, possibly including the use of full-time thanatologists [thanatology is the study of death and dying] specially trained for the act.

Psychiatric Patients Should Be Empowered, Not Protected

Most likely, the taboo against assisted suicide for the mentally ill is a well-meaning yet misplaced response to the long history of mistreatment that those with psychiatric illness have endured in western societies. Psychiatrists and mental health advocates may fear that their patients will be coerced to "choose death" against their wishes, or that, once suicide is an acceptable option, the care for those who reject assisted suicide will be diminished. But as the plaintiff argued before the Swiss high court, in challenging "medical paternalism," we are entering an era during which psychiatric patients do not need to be protected, but empowered. Our goal should be to maximize the options available to the mentally ill.

The Swiss case is not the first in which a nation's high court has suggested a right to suicide for those with mood disorders. In 1993, the Dutch Supreme Court refused to impose a penalty on psychiatrist Boudewijn Chabot for assisting in the suicide of his patient, Hilly Bosscher, a chronically depressed fifty-year-old woman who insisted she did not wish to continue living after the death of both of her adult sons. Boudewijn nevertheless received a reprimand from his local medical disciplinary tribunal, creating a strong civil deterrent for others to follow his lead. The Bosscher case arose when the euthanasia movement was still in its infancy, however. Since assisted suicide for the terminally ill was itself taboo fifteen years ago, it was unrealistic to expect that a mainstream debate would arise over the issue of suicide rights for psychiatric patients. But now that several Western nations and one U.S. state have liberalized their laws, it seems reasonable to question the policies that universally deny such a basic opportunity to the mentally ill.

| "Assisted suicide for someone with depression would be utterly wrong."

It Is Immoral to Give People Suffering from Mental Illness a Choice to Die

Lewis Wolpert

In the following viewpoint, Lewis Wolpert insists that assisted suicide should not be made available to people suffering with depression. Wolpert supports assisted suicide as an option for people with terminal illnesses. However, he says depression is very different. Depressive thoughts are not rational, says Wolpert, and most importantly depression can be cured. Lewis Wolpert is a noted English biologist. He wrote about his own experience with depression in Malignant Sadness: The Anatomy of Depression.

As you read, consider the following questions:

1. According to Wolpert, what is the name of the Swiss euthanasia clinic that wants to offer assisted suicide to the mentally ill?

2. According to Wolpert, who described assisted suicide as an "emergency exit" for those suffering from mental illness? What is this person's job?

3. Why does Wolpert think cognitive therapy worked so well in treating his depression?

One morning, when I was 65-years-old, I woke from a broken night's sleep with an overwhelming desire to kill myself. I had a happy marriage and a rewarding career but I had been depressed for a while and, that day, I truly wanted to die. I woke my wife to tell her how I felt, my daughter came to help and within hours I was in the Royal Free Hospital in London.

Depression Made Me Want to Kill Myself

Twelve years on, I still don't fully understand what caused my depression. I was having some minor problems with my heart at the time and I believe my fears about that may have played a part. I had changed medication and gone badly down hill so was deeply anxious about my health. I couldn't sleep and could barely summon the energy to get out of bed. I saw a psychiatrist who put me on anti-depressant drugs known as tri-cyclics, but they didn't work.

I was reminded of that terrible time when I read yesterday that Ludwig Minelli, who runs the Swiss euthanasia clinic Dignitas, wants to offer the 'marvellous possibility' of assisted suicide not only to the terminally ill but to people with mental illnesses, including clinical depression.

In the darkest days of my own depression, a pact with my wife was the only thing that prevented me from taking my own life. At my lowest points, I thought a lot about how I might kill myself.

I was rational enough to know that I wanted a pain-free method guaranteed to work. I know that if a Swiss clinic had been offering such a service to patients with depression, I would certainly have thought about it. I believe that my responsibility to my family would have prevented me from going any further, but many sufferers do not have that barrier.

Any suggestion that assisted suicide is a justifiable option for people with depression is wrong, and I am horrified by Minelli's proposal.

Depression Is Different than Terminal Illness

I am totally for voluntary euthanasia for those with terminal illnesses. In cases where there is no hope of recovery and the quality of living can only deteriorate, I think people should be able to choose the time of their death and be given the opportunity to spend their last hours with their loved ones instead of in agony or on a life-support machine. But depression is not a terminal illness.

First, terminally ill patients must be able to prove that they have made their decision rationally and without the influence of any other party in order to be allowed to have an assisted suicide at Dignitas. People who are severely depressed are simply not capable of making decisions like that.

Second, there is an important distinction to be made between voluntary euthanasia, where someone is assisted in bringing nearer an end that is already inevitable, and suicide—which is driven by depressive feelings.

By the time I was hospitalised I'd been depressed for a while but nothing could have prepared me for the despair I was feeling. I was put on Seroxat (one of a group of antidepressants known as Selective Serotonin Re-Uptake Inhibitors) and I remained in hospital for about three weeks. I also underwent cognitive therapy, which teaches you ways to break the pattern of negative thinking. Eventually, I improved enough to go home.

I still felt terrible and was unable to escape the suicidal thoughts, and this was when my wife made a deal with me. We would wait for a year, and if I still felt that I wanted to die, she would help me to do it. Tragically, my wife died of cancer two years later but, though it seems a terrible thing to say, for me, the depression was worse than losing my wife. That's how dreadful it can be.

In his speech at at the Liberal Democrat conference in Brighton on Wednesday, Minelli described assisted suicide as "emergency exit" for those suffering from mental illness, and spoke of a test case involving a patient with bi-polar disorder (manic depression) who is fighting for the right to die at the clinic. [The case was heard in the Swiss Supreme court in Fall, 2006.]

Knowing all that I do about what it is like to have severe depression, this idea of an "emergency exit" appalls me. In spite of the overwhelming power of my desire to commit suicide, I never attempted it, and eventually, the depression that had consumed me so completely began to lift. Surely this is all the evidence required to prove that assisted suicide for someone with depression would be utterly wrong.

Depression Is Curable

Many people who feel as I did do try to kill themselves, and succeed. But having depression doesn't mean you are going to die. It can hit you when you are young and healthy, with the whole of your life ahead of you. It is utterly devastating while you are in it, and you can be convinced that it will never end, but evidence shows that almost every case of depression is self-limiting, and it is curable.

Cognitive therapy and anti-depressants worked for me, but everyone has to find the best treatment for them. For some it might be prayer, for others it could be meditation or psychotherapy; it's a devastating illness but one with a great many effective forms of treatment.

There is some evidence that the more you understand about the treatment, the better you do, which I think is why cognitive therapy worked so well for me. You don't have to understand how your brain works, or what is happening to it

Depression Can Make You Feel Like Suicide Is the Only Answer

What a lot of people who have never experienced a serious depression or suicidal thoughts don't understand is how could someone feel so hopeless and depressed to consider ending their entire life? The answer is often rooted in how hopeless and endless the depression seems to be. People who are suicidal are usually in the grips of a serious and untreated (or undertreated) depressive episode. Many people can hide such emotional pain very well, and pretend to be okay. But underneath, they may be in extreme agony and in need of help.

A big part of depression is thinking *irrationally*. This means a person is putting together the pieces of their life in a way that wouldn't make sense to most others. There is an overemphasis on some pieces or some feelings that others would think are being blown out of proportion. But someone who is depressed often can't think any differently—the depression is causing them to emphasize or focus on things that only contribute to the depression. This creates a snowball effect that often lands someone who is seriously depressed at the door of considering suicide.

The key to stopping the snowball effect before it's too late is to acknowledge the pain and agony, and get help.

John Grohol, "What Is Suicide," PsychCentral.com, March 26, 2007.

biologically; all you need to see is what triggers the depression and how to find a way of managing it.

The difficulty when writing about depression is that when one is clinically depressed, one enters a state that is indescribable. It seems extraordinary that, despite the fact that 10–20 per cent of the population have a depressive episode at some point in their lives, there's not one novel I know of that properly portrays it. But I think there is a reason for that; if you can describe severe depression then you haven't had it.

Despite this—and even to those people whose depression has recurred throughout their lives, or who feel that the severity of their illness makes life meaningless—I would offer my own case as an example.

I now want to live as ardently as I once wanted to die. Suicide, assisted or otherwise, would have been the wrong path to take.

Periodical Bibliography

The following articles have been selected to supplement the diverse views presented in this chapter.

Kathleen M. Foley   "Is Physician-Assisted Suicide Ever Acceptable? It's Never Acceptable," *Family Practice News.* June 1, 2007.

Patrick Goodenough   "Study Defending Assisted Suicide Written by Assisted Suicide Advocate," CNSNews.com. September 28, 2007. Available at www.cnsnews.com/.

Joanne Kenen   "In Search of a Gentler End," *Stateline.org.* October 29, 2007. Available at www.stateline.org.

Steven Moffic   "Dr. Death and the Meaning of Life," *Clinical Psychiatry News.* September, 2007.

Timothy E. Quill   "Is Physician-Assisted Suicide Ever Acceptable? It's Justified in Rare Cases," *Family Practice News.* June 1, 2007.

Kevin Sack   "In Hospice Care, Longer Lives Mean Money Lost," *New York Times.* November 27, 2007.

Mary Shaw   "The Other Pro-Choice Movement," Common dreams.org. January 21, 2006. Available at http://www.commondreams.org/views06/0121-23.htm

Liz Townsend   "Officials Work to Prevent Onstage Suicide at Rock Concert," *National Right to Life News.* October 2003.

For Further Discussion

Chapter 1

1. Michael Jellinek contends that teens are most at risk of suicide, while the *Native American Report* asserts that Native American teens are particularly vulnerable to suicide. Do these authors agree upon anything? If so, what?

2. Linda Chaudron and Eric Caine say the suicide risk faced by women receives little attention, while Henry O'Connell, Ai-Vyrn Chin, Conal Cunningham, and Brian A. Lawlor say that the risk of suicide faced by the elderly receives little attention. Why do you think the amount of attention a certain group receives in relation to suicide research is important? Explain.

3. After reading Peter LaBarbera's viewpoint about gay suicide, do you think the statistic that 30 percent of all completed teen suicide attempts involve gay, lesbian, and transgender youths is accurate or inaccurate? Explain. Use examples from the viewpoint to support your position.

4. After reading the viewpoints in Chapter 1, which group of people do you think has the greatest risk of suicide? Why? Use examples from the viewpoints to support your position.

Chapter 2

1. Sundararajan Rajagopal sites suicide chat rooms and other Interact Web sites as a possible cause of increased suicides. However, Brian Mishara and David Weisstub say there isn't enough data to prove this contention and that these Internet Web sites should not be censored. Do you

believe these Web sites cause suicide? How would you deal with these Web sites? Would you censor them? Why or why not?

2. Kevin Caruso contends that Accutane causes depression and suicides, while Michael Fumento argues that the acne medication has gotten a bad rap. Whose argument do you think is stronger and why? Do you think Accutane causes suicide? Why or why not?

3. Alan Dershowitz contends that Islamic fundamentalism causes suicide terrorism, but Robert Pape disagrees. What does Dershowitz think would happen to suicide terrorists if U.S. troops left Iraq? What does Pape think would happen to suicide terrorists if the United States left Iraq? Whose argument do you agree with, and why?

Chapter 3

1. Ed Edelson writes about a study that concludes that antidepressants prevent suicide, while Peter Breggin says that antidepressants cause suicidal behavior, and Robert Bazell says the truth is somewhere in between. What statements does Bazell make that corroborate Edelson's viewpoint? Do any corroborate Breggin's viewpoint? Do any of Bazell's points counter statements from Edelson or Breggin?

2. Richard A. Friedman thinks school-based suicide screening programs such as Teen Screen can prevent teen suicide. However Ellen Liversidge, says Teen Screen is a deceptive tool used by the pharmaceutical industry to sell antidepressants. Whose viewpoint do you think was more persuasive? Do you think that teens should be screened for mental health problems as Friedman does? Or do you agree with Liversidge, that screening programs don't work and are designed to sell antidepressants? Support your conclusion with examples from the viewpoints.

3. Chris Korda believes that suicide is an acceptable method to decrease the threat that humans cause to the earth. Do you think he has a legitimate point? Do you think a substantial number of people agree with Korda? Explain.

Chapter 4

1. Compare and contrast Kathryn Tucker's viewpoint that people should be allowed to choose physician-assisted suicide with Diane Coleman's viewpoint that giving people the right to choose assisted suicide is harmful to disabled people. Coleman and Tucker both cite the same reasons for why people might want to hasten their death, but they each have different perceptions about the validity of these reasons. Why do you think this is so? How do their past experiences shade their viewpoint? Compare and contrast each author's impression of doctors. How does their impression of doctors influence their viewpoint?

2. Wesley J. Smith believes physician-assisted suicide devalues life and inevitably leads to justified killing of the poor, the disabled, and the elderly, while Garret Keizer contends that physician-assisted suicide does not devalue life and will not lead to justified killing of the weak in society. How do you think each author would answer the question, "what does it mean to be human and be alive?" Explain.

3. Jacob Appel believes that people suffering from severe depression should be able to choose assisted suicide, while Lewis Wolpert insists they should not have this option. Whose argument do you agree with, and why?

4. After reading the viewpoints in this chapter, do you support physician-assisted suicide? Do you think the right to choose the time and manner of one's death is a human right? Explain why or why not.

Organizations to Contact

The editors have compiled the following list of organizations concerned with the issues debated in this book. The descriptions are derived from materials provided by the organizations. All have publications or information available for interested readers. The list was compiled on the date of publications of the present volume; the information provided here may change. Be aware that many organizations may take several weeks or longer to respond to inquiries, so allow as much time as possible.

Alliance for Human Research Protection
142 West End Avenue, Suite 28P, New York, NY   10023
Web site: www.ahrp.org

The Alliance for Human Research Protection is a national network of lay people and professionals dedicated to advancing responsible and ethical medical research practices and exposing corruption in the field of health care. The group speaks out against the widespread prescribing of antidepressants and other drugs. They publish an online infomail containing news articles about medical fraud and corruption.

American Association of Suicidology (AAS)
5221 Wisconsin Avenue NW, Washington, DC   20015
(202) 237-2280 • fax: (202) 237-2282
e-mail: info@suicidology.org
Web site: www.suicidology.org

The American Association of Suicidology (AAS) is a nonprofit suicide prevention organization founded by psychologist Edwin Shneidman. The AAS provides training, education, services, and support for mental health workers, crisis center staff, and those who have lost a loved one to suicide. AAS publishes *Suicide and Life-Threatening Behavior*, a monthly peer-reviewed journal, *Surviving Suicide*, a quarterly newsletter, and several other publications.

American Foundation for Suicide Prevention

120 Wall Street, 22nd Fl., New York, NY 10005
(212) 363-3500 • fax: (212) 363-6237
e-mail: inquiry@afsp.org
Web site: www.afsp.org

The American Foundation for Suicide Prevention is a national nonprofit organization dedicated to funding the research, education, and treatment programs necessary to prevent suicide. The AFSP also provides resources and support to suicide survivors and publishes various suicide prevention and survivor support pamphlets, books, and brochures.

Compassion & Choices

PO Box 101810, Denver, CO 80250-1810
(800) 247-7421 • fax: (303) 639-1224
e-mail: info@compassionandchoices.org
Web site: www.compassionandchoices.org

Compassion & Choices is a nonprofit organization working to legalize physician-assisted suicide and improve end-of-life care. Compassion & Choices was originally founded as the Hemlock Society in 1980. The organization seeks to change U.S. laws to expand choices at the end of life. It publishes the quarterly *Compassion and Choices Magazine.*

International Task Force on Euthanasia and Assisted Suicide

PO Box 760, Steubenville, OH 43952
(740) 282-3810
Web site: www.internationaltaskforce.org

The International Task Force on Euthanasia and Assisted Suicide is a nonprofit organization that opposes physician-assisted suicide and euthanasia. The organization seeks to influence public policy and educate people about the dangers of physician-assisted suicide and euthanasia. It publishes a periodical news magazine called the *Update.*

Mental Health America

2000 N Beauregard Street, 6th Fl., Alexandria, VA   22311
(703) 684-7722 • fax: (703) 684-5968
Web site: www.mentalhealthamerica.net

Mental Health America (formerly known as the National Mental Health Association) is a nonprofit organization dedicated to helping all people live mentally healthier lives. The organization educates the public about ways to preserve and strengthen its mental health; fights for access to effective mental health care; fights to end discrimination against people with mental and addictive disorders; and fosters innovative mental health research, treatment, and support services. Mental Health America issues several e-mail newsletters, such as *The Bell*, and produces several fact sheets and informational documents.

National Alliance on Mental Illness (NAMI)

2107 Wilson Blvd., Ste. 300, Arlington, VA   22201-3042
(703) 524-7600 • fax: (703) 524-9094
e-mail: info@nami.org
Web site: www.nami.org

The National Alliance on Mental Illness (NAMI) is a national grassroots mental health organization that seeks to eradicate mental illness and improve the lives of persons living with serious mental illness and their families. NAMI works through advocacy, research, education, and support. The organization publishes a periodic magazine called the *Advocate*.

Screening for Mental Health, Inc.

One Washington Street, Ste. 304, Wellesley Hills, MA   02481
(781) 239-0071 • fax: (781) 431-7447
e-mail: smhinfo@mentalhealthscreening.org
Web site: www.mentalhealthscreening.org

Screening for Mental Health, Inc. is a nonprofit organization that develops and administers large-scale mental health screenings, such as the SOS Signs of Suicide High School Program and National Depression Screening Day. The organization seeks to identify people with mental illness and help them to seek treatment. The organization produces various FAQs and other educational materials about suicide, alcoholism, and depression.

Substance Abuse and Mental Health Services Administration (SAMHSA)
1 Choke Cherry Road, Rockville, MD   20857

The Substance Abuse and Mental Health Services Administration (SAMHSA), part of the U.S. Department of Health and Human Services (HHS), seeks to ensure that people who suffer from mental health or substance abuse disorders have the opportunity to live fulfilling and meaningful lives. The agency's vision is expressed with "A Life in the Community for Everyone." SAMHSA works to expand and enhance prevention and early intervention programs and improve the quality, availability, and range of mental health and substance abuse treatment and support services in local communities across the United States. The agency publishes a bimonthly newsletter, *SAMSHA News*, as well as various recurring statistical reports on mental health and substance abuse.

Suicide Awareness Voices of Education
8120 Penn Avenue S Ste. 470, Bloomington, MN   55431
(952) 946-7998
Web site: www.save.org

Suicide Awareness Voices of Education is a nonprofit organization dedicated to preventing suicide through public awareness and education, reducing the stigma of mental illness, and serving as a resource to the survivors of suicide. The organization publishes a newsletter three times a year, which provides information on suicide prevention, depression, and coping with suicide.

Suicide Prevention Action Network USA
1025 Vermont Avenue NW; Suite 1066
Washington, DC   20005
(202) 449-3600 • fax: (202) 449-3601
e-mail: info@spanusa.org
Web site: www.spanusa.org

The Suicide Prevention Action Network is a nonprofit organization dedicated to preventing suicide through public education and awareness, community action and federal, state, and
local grassroots advocacy. The organization publishes a quarterly newsletter and several booklets, brochures, and fact sheets
about suicide prevention.

Bibliography of Books

Books

Pabst M. Battin

Ending Life: Ethics and the Way We Die. New York: Oxford University Press, 2005.

Nigel Biggar

Aiming to Kill: The Ethics of Suicide and Euthanasia. Cleveland: Pilgrim Press, 2004.

Susan Rose Blauner

How I Stayed Alive When My Brain Was Trying to Kill Me: One Person's Guide to Suicide Prevention. New York: Harper Paperbacks, 2003.

Mia Bloom

Dying to Kill: The Allure of Suicide Terror. New York: Columbia University Press, 2005.

Francis Chalifour

After. Toronto: Tundra Books, 2005.

Bev Cobain and Jean Larch

Dying to Be Free: A Healing Guide for Families After a Suicide. Center City, MN: Hazelden, 2006.

David Cox and Candy Arrington

Aftershock: Help, Hope, and Healing in the Wake of Suicide. Nashville, TN: B&H Publishing Group, 2003.

Emile Durkheim, Richard Sennet, Alexander Riley, and Robin Buss

On Suicide. New York: Penguin Classics, 2007.

Wanda Dyson	*Dramatic Rescue & Return to Hope.* Grand Rapids, MI: Fleming H. Revell, 2006.
Heather Hays	*Surviving Suicide: Help to Heal Your Heart—Life Stories from Those Left Behind.* Dallas, TX: Brown Books, 2005.
Ronald M. and Stephen Holmes	*Suicide: Theory, Practice, and Investigation.* Thousand Oaks, CA: Sage Publications, 2006.
Derek Humphry	*Final Exit: The Practicalities of Self-deliverance and Assisted Suicide for the Dying.* New York: Delta Books, 2003.
Tom Hunt	*Cliffs of Despair: A Journey to Suicide's Edge.* New York: Random House, 2006.
Kay Redfield Jamison	*Night Falls Fast: Understanding Suicide.* Washington, DC: Dana Press Books, 2000.
Thomas Joiner	*Why People Die by Suicide.* Cambridge, MA: Harvard University Press, 2005.
Jon Klimo and Pamela Heath	*Suicide: What Really Happens in the Afterlife?* Berkeley, CA: North Atlantic Books, 2006.
Mark M. Leach	*Cultural Diversity and Suicide: Ethnic, Religious, Gender, and Sexual Orientation Perspectives.* New York: Haworth Press, 2006.

Christopher Lukas and Henry M. Seiden
Silent Grief: Living in the Wake of Suicide. Philadelphia, PA: Jessica Kingsley Publishers, 2007.

Hal Marcovitz
Teens and Suicide. Philadelphia, PA: Mason Crest Publishers, 2004.

Viola Mecke
Fatal Attachments: The Instigation to Suicide. Westport, CT: Praeger, 2004.

Michael F. Myers and Carla Fine
Touched by Suicide: Hope and Healing After a Loss. New York: Gotham Books, 2006.

Neal Nicol and Harry Wylie
Between the Dying and the Dead: Dr. Jack Kevorkian's Life and the Battle to Legalize Euthanasia. Madison, WI: University of Wisconsin Press/Terrace Books, 2006.

Richard E. Nelson, Judith C. Galas, and Bev Cobain
The Power to Prevent Suicide: A Guide for Teens Helping Teens. Minneapolis, MN: Free Spirit Pub., 2006.

Ami Pedahzur
Root Causes of Suicide Terrorism: The Globalization of Martyrdom. New York: Routledge, 2006.

Barry Rosenfeld
Assisted Suicide and the Right to Die: The Interface of Social Science, Public Policy, and Medical Ethics. Washington, DC: American Psychological Association, 2004.

Edwin S. Shneidman
Autopsy of a Suicidal Mind. New York: Oxford University Press, 2004.

Gordon H. Smith   *Remembering Garrett: One Family's Battle with a Child's Depression.* New York: Carroll & Graf, 2006.

Kate Sofronoff,   *Out of Options: A Cognitive Model of*
Len Dalgliesh,   *Adolescent Suicide and Risk Taking.*
and Robert Kosky   New York: Cambridge University Press, 2005.

United States   *A Generation at Risk: Breaking the*
Senate Special   *Cycle of Senior Suicide: Hearing Be-*
Committee on   *fore the Special Committee on Aging,*
Aging   *United States Senate 109th Congress.* Washington, DC: G.P.O., 2006.

United States   *Indian Youth Suicide: Hearing Before*
Senate Committee   *the Committee on* Indian Affairs,
on Indian Affairs   United States Senate 109th Congress. Washington, DC: G.P.O., 2006.

Belinda Woolley,   *"If Only. . .: Personal Stories of Loss*
Ed.   *Through Suicide,"* Australia: University of Western Australia Press, 2006.

Index

Date Due →	10/25/12		
Books returned after due date are subject to a fine.	4/9/13		